The World Book of
AMERICA'S MULTICULTURAL HERITAGE

World Book, Inc.

a Scott Fetzer company

Chicago

STAFF

President
Robert C. Martin

Editorial

Managing Editor
Maureen Mostyn Liebenson

Senior Editor
Shawn Brennan

Contributing Editor
Lisa Klobuchar

Writer
James I. Clark

Permissions Editor
Janet T. Peterson

Indexing Services
David Pofelski, *head*
Tina Trettin

Cartographic Services
George Stoll, *head*
Wayne Pichler

Art

Executive Director
Roberta Dimmer

Art Director
Wilma Stevens

Senior Designer
Cari Biamonte

Photography Manager
Sandra M. Dyrlund

Photographs Editor
Sylvia Ohlrich

Production Assistant
John Whitney

Research

**Executive Director,
Product Development
and Research Services**
Paul A. Kobasa

**Manager, Research
Services**
Loranne K. Shields

**Chief Researcher,
Special Projects**
Cheryl Graham

Production

**Director, Manufacturing
and Pre-Press**
Carma Fazio

Manager, Manufacturing
Barbara Podczerwinski

Senior Production Manager
Madelyn Underwood

**Production/Technology
Manager**
Jared Svoboda

Proofreader
Anne Dillon

Text Processing
Curley Hunter
Gwendolyn Johnson

Consultants

Carol Berkin
Professor of History
Baruch College and CUNY
Graduate Center
New York, New York

Philip Lax
President
Ellis Island Restoration
Commission
New York, New York

World Book, Inc.
233 N. Michigan Avenue
Chicago, Illinois 60601

For information about other World Book publications, visit our Web site **http: www.worldbook.com**, or call **1-800-WORLDBK** (967-5325). For information about sales to schools and libraries, call **1-800-975-3250 (United States)**; **1-800-837-5365 (Canada)**.

Printed in Singapore
1 2 3 4 5 6 7 09 08 07 06 05 04 03

Library of Congress Cataloging-in-Publication Data

The World Book of America's multicultural heritage.
   p. cm
   Rev. ed. of: The World Book of America's heritage. c1991.
   Includes index.
   ISBN 0-7166-7303-7
    1. United States–History. 2. Ethnology–United States.
3. Immigrants–United States–History. 4. United States–
Emigration and immigration–History. I. World Book, Inc. II.
World Book of America's heritage.

E178.W8995 2003
973'.04–dc21   2002193358

This work was previously published under the title *The World Book of America's Heritage* © 1991.

PREFACE

The World Book of America's Multicultural Heritage celebrates the rich diversity of people who proudly call themselves Americans. These books tell the powerful stories of groups and individuals who struggled to make better lives for themselves and their descendants.

Using a chronological format, the books present all the various groups of Americans, beginning with the earliest immigrants, who came across the Bering Strait from Asia many thousands of years ago. Volume 1 presents the people who arrived before 1800 — the Indians, European explorers, Pilgrims, colonists, Loyalists, and Patriots. The book also sensitively portrays the plight of those unwilling immigrants, the Africans who were brought to the Western Hemisphere as slaves.

Volume 2 tells the lively story of the westward movement and the growth of America as a nation as the result of the Northwest Ordinance, the Louisiana Purchase, and the Mexican Cession. The book highlights the immigrants who came through Ellis Island and describes the restoration of that historic place. The volume continues with events in the late 20th and early 21st centuries, including the appearance of new immigrant groups and the effects all groups have on one another.

Through the use of lavish illustrations and the words of the immigrants themselves, the reader can get the full impact of what it meant to be an American at different times in history. Maps also help point out where major events took place.

The World Book of America's Multicultural Heritage also carefully explores the darker side of immigration through discussions of racial prejudice, discriminatory laws, and the sometimes-violent confrontations that have occurred between groups or individuals.

A number of feature pages in each volume are also devoted to interesting historical sites, special world events, or noteworthy people. These include New Salem, Ill., the development of sailing ships, and the American expatriates. Also highlighted in special sections are the immigration movements to Canada, Hawaii, and Alaska.

The World Book of America's Multicultural Heritage presents the pageant of America's people — their joys and sorrows, their successes and failures. Here, in words and pictures, are the stories of those who have become known as Americans.

CONTENTS

Book One

Book Two

PART 1: THE LAND AND ITS FIRST PEOPLE

For millions of years during the earth's early
history, the Western Hemisphere, like the rest of the
world, remained without humans. It is now believed
that the first people came from Asia only 20,000 to
25,000 years ago. Their descendants eventually spread
out over both continents, each group developing a
culture that reflected the environment in which it
settled.

*The dramatic Teton
Mountains tower
over the Snake River
in what is today
northwestern Wyo-
ming. In 1929, the
area was designated
as Grand Teton Na-
tional Park.*

7

Storm clouds gather over Badlands National Park. The area was made a national monument in 1929 and a national park in 1978.

CHAPTER 1: THE GLORIOUS CONTINENTS

Most scientists believe the earliest people came to what is now Alaska from Siberia across a land bridge that existed as recently as 10,000 years ago. In the vast stretches of what is now North America and South America, these early immigrants found their new homes to be a land of great beauty and incredible contrasts.

The wide variety of animals and plants in North America includes the arctic wolf, the hardy fireweed plant, and the bald eagle, the national bird of the United States.

Tundra. From Alaska across the breadth of Canada just south of the Arctic Circle lies a cold, treeless region of desert called *tundra*. During the long winters, temperatures fall very low and stay there a long time. During much of the winter, the sun remains below the horizon, making the tundra for a time a land of darkness. This forbidding climate is such that the tundra remains permanently frozen just a few inches below the surface. Animal life on the tundra consists mainly of polar bears, white-furred arctic foxes, a few ptarmigans, snowy owls, and some rodents. With the beginning of the brief summer, the region suddenly comes alive as a

Many animals such as this arctic hare inhabit the tundra areas near Mount McKinley in Alaska. Sometimes called the top of the continent *because of its height, Mount McKinley is the chief scenic at-traction of Denali National Park.*

few top inches of the permanently fro-zen ground—permafrost—thaws. Musk oxen, caribou, and a myriad of birds return from their winter quarters in the south, and hundreds of kinds of quick-growing flowers brighten the landscape. In September, the tran-sients leave. Soon the cold silence of the Arctic winter envelopes the land again.

South of the tundra lies a vast for-est region. Extending from Alaska across the continent to the Atlantic and south in places to slightly beyond the northern border of the present-day United States, this land of spruce, fir, hemlock, and pine is home to black bears, wolves, wolverines, moose, lynx, and many kinds of songbirds.

One of the more unusual sights in the coniferous forest zone is a series of huge circular holes, many of them filled with water. These holes are me-teor craters. Most scientists believe they were formed about 500,000,000 years ago. At that time, so the theory goes, a planet somewhere between Mars and Saturn exploded. The larger pieces formed the asteroid belt that still orbits the sun. Other, smaller pieces drifted through space and eventually reached the earth. There, they hit the surface with a tremendous wallop, shattering themselves and gouging out craters in the ground. The largest of these craters thus far discovered — the New Quebec Crater (also known as the Chubb Crater), in Canada — measures 2.1 miles (3.4 kilometers) across.

The pine forests line the western side of the Coast Ranges, a series of mountain ranges that extend from Alaska to southern California. Included is the Alaska Range, with mighty Mount McKinley. At 20,320 feet (6,194 meters) above sea level, it

ters) of rain on the peninsula each year. The resulting rain forest is a tangle of vines and other vegetation as dense and varied as any in the tropics. Sitka spruce trees on the peninsula grow 300 feet (90 meters) tall, redcedars measure 21 feet (6.3 meters) around, and the largest Douglas fir has a diameter of 18 feet (5.4 meters).

Near the northern California border, redwood trees dominate the landscape. More, along with equally ancient sequoias, are also found farther south in the moist, foggy region of the Monterey Peninsula. Redwoods and sequoias are tall, magnificent trees of almost unbelievable age. Annual

---

> ## Snow atop McKinley, as well as in numerous high valleys in western Canada and Alaska, feeds glaciers in the area.

---

is the highest peak in North America. Snow atop McKinley, as well as in numerous high valleys in western Canada and in Alaska, feeds the glaciers in the area. With a few breaks, such as Puget Sound, in the state of Washington and San Francisco Bay, in California, the Coast Ranges continue south from the Olympic Peninsula into Baja California.

Tall Trees. Nestled against the breaking sea and harboring some of North America's tallest and oldest trees, the temperate climate of the Olympic Peninsula of today's Washington state seems out of place. Rising over the Olympic Mountains, westerly winds off the Pacific Ocean bring moisture-heavy clouds that shed an average of 135 inches (343 centime-

rings on one old redwood show an age of 2,200 years. Some sequoias are more than 3,000 years old, and they may live that many years longer.

The Moving Earth. The San Andreas Fault runs through the Coast Ranges in California. (A *fault* is a break in the earth's crust where earthquakes are likely to happen.) The restless mountains of the Coast Ranges have long been subject to earthquakes. Some of these quakes are just slight tremors. Others are major upheavals that produce devastating changes in the earth.

However, the San Andreas Fault is not the only volatile feature of the area. Somewhat inland, the Cascade Mountain Range runs from Washington south to northern California.

Yosemite National Park lies in the Sierra Nevada mountains, about 200 miles (320 kilometers) east of San Francisco, Calif. The park is named for the Yosemite Indians who once lived there.

These volcanic mountains include such peaks as Washington's snow-capped Mount Rainier, rising to 14,410 feet (4,392 meters), and Mount Hood in Oregon, at 11,239 feet (3,426 meters). The volcanic cone of Mount Mazama in Oregon collapsed in the ancient past. Today it forms the bottom of Crater Lake, an icy body of water nearly 2,000 feet (600 meters) deep.

No volcano in the Cascades was active for many years. Then on May 18, 1980, Mount Saint Helens erupted. Located in southwestern Washington, the volcano spewed ash, other debris, and steam high into the atmosphere. The eruption created a cloud of ash that circled the earth. It left 57 people dead and destroyed bridges, roads, trees, and crops in a huge surrounding area.

In California, the Cascades overlook the Sacramento and San Joaquin valleys — the Central Valley — cradled by the Coast Ranges on the west and the Sierra Nevada mountains on the east. This long and remarkably fertile valley system extends south nearly to the present-day city of Los Angeles. The Sacramento and San Joaquin rivers, along with the Yuba, the American, the Merced, and others flowing out of the Sierra Nevada, added to the valley's richness with the sediments they deposited during floodtimes.

Thousands of glacial lakes and many waterfalls dotted the Cascades. At one point, a huge glacier in the Merced River Valley was stranded high above the streams that served the Merced. After the glacier melted, those streams rejoined the Merced by means of waterfalls, including the scenic Upper and Lower Yosemite Falls, which drop a total of 2,425 feet (739 meters) to the Merced River. Yosemite Falls ranks among the 10 highest in North America. Another, Ribbon Falls, tumbles freely for 1,612 feet (491 meters).

Deserts. The Cascades wring out most of the precipitation that passing clouds hold. As a result, the land east of the mountains is semiarid or desert, usually getting 10 inches (25 centimeters) of rainfall or less each year. The largest dry area, now called the Great Basin Desert, covers most of the present-day states of Nevada and Utah. Sagebrush, along with a few cottonwoods and willows along streams, are the only natural vegetation of the Great Basin region. Within it, an ancient lake eventually shrank, creating the Great Salt Lake.

To the southwest is an arid region now called the Painted Desert. Here, wind and rain erosion carved the volcanic rock into buttes, pinnacles, valleys, and mesas. A combination of heat, sunlight, and dust in the air sometimes seems to create the colors of yellow, russet, and red in the soil.

Also in the southwest is the Mojave Desert, with its weird, twisted Joshua trees. The area of the desert aptly named Death Valley, at 282 feet (86 meters) below sea level, is the lowest spot on the continent. Temperatures above 125 °F (52 °C) are common there. A mere 2 inches

Death Valley National Monument in east-central California was established in 1933. Joshua Tree National Monument in southern California was established in 1936. In 1994, both areas were expanded and designated national parks.

(5 centimeters) per year is the maximum rainfall that Death Valley receives.

South of the Mojave, the Sonora Desert extends into modern-day Mexico. Here the sentinellike saguaro cactus has long predominated. Caterpillars, silverfish, lizards, and spiders like to call this cactus "home." East of the Sonora, the Chihuaha Desert, where agave cactus thrives, also extends into Mexico.

The Rockies.

Millions of years ago, subterranean convulsions and upthrustings along fault lines heaved up what are known today as the Rocky Mountains. The chain extends north into Alaska as the Brooks Range. The Sierra Madre Occidental is an extension of the Rockies in Mexico.

The Rockies are not one but many ranges, and those who labeled the ranges gave them intriguing names — Bitterroot, Wind River, Grand Teton, and Beaverhead, to list but a few. Valley glaciers characterize the northern Rockies, particularly in Canada. In a section of the Rockies set aside in the 1800's as Yellowstone National Park are pots of boiling mud, hot-water pools, vents of steam, and geysers. Old Faithful, born perhaps 300 years ago, is the premier geyser. On average, it spews out a stream of boiling water more than 100 feet (30 meters) high every 73 minutes.

Continental Divide.

A major dividing line for the continent's rivers is the Rockies. Those on the west side of the Continental Divide eventually become part of the Pacific Ocean. The mighty rivers on this western side include the Snake, for example, which cuts deep gorges in the land as it races to join the Columbia on its journey to the sea. The mighty Colorado River, along with rain and wind, carved out what is known today as the

Yellowstone National Park is the oldest national park in the world and the largest wildlife preserve in the United States.

Grand Canyon. This wonder of nature is more than a mile deep and sometimes 18 miles (28.8 kilometers) wide.

Equally great rivers formed east of the Continental Divide. For example, the Missouri formed about 20 million years ago and flows east for hundreds of miles before joining the Mississippi on its way to the sea.

The Plains.

A vast and grassy plain developed on the eastern side of the Rockies. Near the mountains, rainfall varying from 10 and 20 inches (25 and 50 centimeters) per year produced short grasses that grew in clumps. This grassy region became the realm of the buffalo. The region was also the province of the burrowing prairie dog, which is actually a rodent. Short grasses gradually gave way to taller prairie grasses as rainfall increased to more than 20 inches (50 centimeters) a year farther east.

Streams flowing down from the Rockies helped shape the plains with their sediment deposits and erosion effects. The Badlands, in what is now South Dakota, are a striking example of that erosion. Here streams cut away soft rock and slowly transformed the more resistant rock into an eerie landscape of ridges, knobs, pinnacles, and canyons.

Forests.

Near the Mississippi, the tall grasses gave way to forests of hardwoods such as oak and maple extending to the low Appalachian Moun-

Grand Canyon National Park, established in 1919, covers an area larger than the state of Rhode Island. About 3 million tourists visit the park each year in northwest Arizona.

Great Smoky Mountains National Park, established in 1930, lies on the boundary between North Carolina and Tennessee. It contains the most extensive virgin hardwood and red spruce forests in the U.S. today.

tains. South of the hardwood forests, a band of longleaf pines and other coniferous trees extended from the Father of Waters, an ancient name for the Mississippi, to the eastern ocean. North of the forested area lay five large bodies of water later named the Great Lakes. Formed about 10,000 to 12,000 years ago by advancing and retreating glaciers, the Great Lakes became a key source of fresh water on the North American continent for all the people who were soon to come.

The **Appalachians.** While the western mountains are merely millions of years old, the rock upheavals that produced the Appalachians took place hundreds of millions of years ago. Wind and rain erosion, as well as glaciers in the northern part, wore the Appalachians down to high, rounded hills. Today, the highest peak reaches only 6,684 feet (2,005.2 meters) above sea level.

The Great Smoky Mountains nurtured the most varied and luxuriant forests in the Appalachians. Low-hanging clouds dropping more than 80 inches (200 centimeters) of precipitation per year, along with fog rising from the valleys, created the humid atmosphere that looks like smoke and gave the mountains their name. The luxuriant region became home to hundreds of kinds of trees and birds.

The **Coastline of the Eastern Ocean.** The eastern coastline of North America is rocky in the north, with a combination of rocky and sandy beaches in the central areas. Fine sandy beaches line the southern coast as far as land extends.

Inland, Lake Okeechobee is an outstanding feature of what is now Florida. Numerous streams flow into the shallow lake, but none flow out, producing a swampy area of 10-foot- (3-meter-) high saw grass known today as the Everglades. The Everglades form a unique area filled with fabulous birds and animals such as crocodiles, alligators, and manatees.

Central and South America.

For millions of years, seas covered what is now Central America and kept North and South America separated. Then, about a million years ago, an intense eruption from beneath the sea floor created a narrow strip of land to connect the two continents. The interior region evolved into a land of rugged mountains, while narrow coastal plains with dense rain forests developed along both coasts.

Uplifted rock and volcanoes formed the Andes Mountains — a vast region of jagged, snow-covered peaks towering over broad, grassy plateaus and glacier-filled valleys. The Andes are the longest mountain range above sea level in the world, running from what is now Venezuela in the north to Tierra del Fuego in the south. Like the Coast Ranges of North America, the Andes lie near the ocean. Only a narrow, mostly dry coastal plain all along its length separates the mountain range from the sea. Also like the Coast Ranges, volcanic eruptions and earthquakes still occur in the Andes region.

East of the Andes, a central plains area covers three-fifths of South America. East of the plains are two highlands areas — the Guiana Highlands in the north and the Brazilian Highlands, occupying nearly a quarter of the continent, in the south. The Amazon River, which with its many

Everglades National Park, established in 1947, is one of the few subtropical regions in the United States. The exotic environment has been threatened in recent decades by massive population growth nearby.

The Caribbean area contains some regions of lush vegetation, such as this one along the east coast of Costa Rica, as well as unusual animals, such as the gentle plant-eating manatee.

tributaries drains the central plain, separates the highland areas. The Amazon itself flows 4,000 miles (6,437 kilometers) from the Peruvian Andes to the Atlantic Ocean, making it the second longest river in the world — only Egypt's Nile is longer.

Two large lakes evolved on the continent. The larger, Lake Maracaibo, covers some 5,217 square miles (13,512 square kilometers) and is in present-day Venezuela. Lake Titicaca, lying some 12,507 feet (3,812 meters) up in the Andes, sits on the border of what is now Peru and Bolivia. The continent's many waterfalls include the spectacular Angel Falls in Venezuela. As the world's highest, Angel Falls plunges 3,212 feet (979 meters).

Varied climates developed in South America. In the lowlands, heavy precipitation throughout the year, plus high temperatures created dense rain forests. This was particularly true in the Amazon River Basin. Lack of rainfall created deserts along the western coast and in the area now known as Patagonia in southern Argentina. A vast grasslands region developed north of Patagonia. Similar to the grasslands interior of North America, this South American region later came to be called the *pampa*.

An impressive variety of animal life evolved in South America, especially in the Amazon River Basin area. This region became home to such exotic creatures as the capybara — the world's largest rodent at about 4 feet (1.2 meters) in length. The manatee, an Amazon water mammal weighing from 700 to 1,000 pounds (315 to 450 kilograms), is also found there, as is the arapaima, a huge freshwater fish that can grow more than 8 feet (2.4 meters) long. Other creatures include many kinds of monkeys, the giant anteater, the sloth, the maned wolf, the llama, the jaguar, swamp deer, and the anaconda, one of the largest snakes in the world.

Abundant plant life also flourished in South America. Edible plants include the pineapple, the avocado, the cassava, and the coconut palm. Medicinal plants include the cinchona, the source of quinine, which is used to treat malaria. Other plants include the balsa tree, which produces a very lightweight wood, and the mahogany tree, which is used in fine furniture.

One of the most valuable food plants of South America is the potato, which originated in the Andes at altitudes above 11,000 feet (3,300 meters). Early inhabitants of Peru used to preserve the potato by a combined freezing and drying technique. After harvesting the crop, they would spread the potatoes on the ground and leave them overnight in the frigid air. The next morning, the villagers would trample on the potatoes to squeeze out their moisture. The villagers would repeat the process for several days until all the moisture was gone. The dried potatoes were then stored.

In the 1500's, the potato was carried to Europe, where it received a mixed reception. In some countries, such as Spain and England, it quickly became popular. People ate it "with good butter, salt, juice of oranges and lemons, and double refined sugar." The French, however, banned it, claiming it caused leprosy. Not until 1806 did a French cookbook finally include a potato recipe.

The Andes Mountains stretch along the entire west coast of South America. Both the llama and its smaller relative the alpaca are well-suited to the arid western slopes found along much of the range.

All early groups made the things they needed out of the materials they had available. The Navajo of the Southwest grew cotton and then wove it into beautiful blankets. The Plains Indians greatly prized the buffalo. Every part of the animal found a use—from food, clothing, housing, and weapons to flyswatters, pillows, and rope.

CHAPTER 2: THE FIRST AMERICANS

Tens of thousands of years ago, glaciers up to two miles thick repeatedly advanced and retreated across northern lands as long periods of cold and warm alternated. In times of intense cold, sometimes lasting thousands of years, water vapor rose from the sea and returned to earth as snow. This process fed the glacial advances. Sometimes the process caused ocean levels to drop.

The Pueblo, also of the Southwest, are well-known for their elegant pottery which frequently has elaborate, geometric patterns for decoration. The cornhusk mask was worn by members of the Husk Face Society, a religious group within the Iroquois nation.

When that happened, the Bering Strait, a sliver of water about 50 miles (80 kilometers) wide separating Asia and North America, became almost entirely dry, and a land bridge developed. Archaeologists have concluded that the first immigrants to the Americas passed over that land bridge. They were the forebears of people known today as American Indians, Native Americans, and Amerindians—three names often used to describe the same groups of people who were early inhabitants of North and South America. Many animals also traveled over the land bridge.

The exact time of this great migration is uncertain. It might have begun as long as 40,000 years ago. The most likely starting time seems to have been about 20,000 years ago. The geological record indicates that a period of advancing glaciation made the Bering Strait into a land bridge beginning around then and that it lasted for several thousand years.

No one today knows what compelled those ancient people to leave their homelands. Possibly they fled before an aggressive people moving onto the Siberian lands from the west. Perhaps they sought more abundant herds of mastodons and hairy mammoths, the huge animals that had long provided them with a key supply of food as well as skins for clothing and shelter. In any case, scholars today believe that these earliest immigrants probably traveled in small bands of 20 to 50 people each.

Over time, the European contact led to the elimination of most facets of the Eskimo life style.

Eskimos had a loose form of government based on rules of conduct that guided their lives and their relations with others. Primarily these rules required that everyone cooperate in the struggle to survive in the harsh environment and to live peaceably with one another.

This struggle to survive revolved around the search for a constant supply of food. Whale, seal, and caribou meat, along with fish, were the principal ingredients of the Eskimo diet. During the short summers, Eskimos also gathered berries and plant roots. They usually ate food raw because their harsh environment gave them

The Eskimos' struggle to survive revolved around the search for a constant supply of food.

Eskimos. The term *Eskimo* is a general term applied by non-Eskimos to a variety of groups. Eskimos call themselves by words meaning *people* —including Inuit in Canada, and Inupiat or Yupik in Alaska.

Instead of migrating south after crossing the Bering land bridge, most of the people that became Eskimos settled in the cold regions of the far north, and gradually spread out from what is now Alaska across Canada to Greenland. Eskimos developed a way of life that enabled them to survive in an area where winter temperatures go well below freezing and stay there for weeks at a time. The traditional Eskimo way of life persisted until they came in contact with Europeans.

little or no fuel for fires. They made lamps of soapstone or animal bones. These burned blubber from seals and whales, but meat took a long time to cook over the low heat such lamps generated.

Eskimos made clothing from the hides of the caribou and whales they caught. In winter the people wore two layers of clothing—an inner layer with fur next to the skin and an outer layer with fur facing out. One layer of clothing was enough for summer months. The harsh climate could cause severe eye problems both from the glare of sunlight on snow and from the wind. To protect their eyes Eskimos made goggles of wood or bone with small holes to see through.

In summer, Eskimos lived in tents made of animal skins. In winter they lived in houses made of sod. They also sometimes cut blocks of hard-packed snow to make winter shelters. By stacking the snow blocks in a continuous, circular row winding upward in ever-smaller circles to form a dome, Eskimos could build a one-room snowhouse in about two hours. Most Eskimos used snowhouses as only temporary quarters. Some groups used them as winter-long housing, though.

Eskimos traveled on foot during the summer. In winter they relied on sleds made of the scarce pieces of wood their environment provided them. Dogs, domesticated over the generations, pulled the sleds. Eskimos traveled on water in two types of boats. One type was a one-person boat called a kayak. The other type was called an umiak and carried 10 to 12 persons. Both types of boats were made of wooden frames covered with animal skins.

Eskimos used kayaks and umiaks to fish, and to hunt seals, whales, and walruses. The Eskimos' principal weapon for hunting water animals was a harpoon with a wooden shaft and a point made of stone or bone. They hunted caribou and other land animals with spears and sometimes with bows and arrows.

The Eskimo language evolved as separately from those of other groups as did other parts of their culture. Unlike most of the world's languages, which can be traced back to a few core languages, the Eskimo one developed

Eskimos built the first kayaks thousands of years ago, often out of sealskin stretched over a wooden frame. The mask is made of bone, feathers, and reeds.

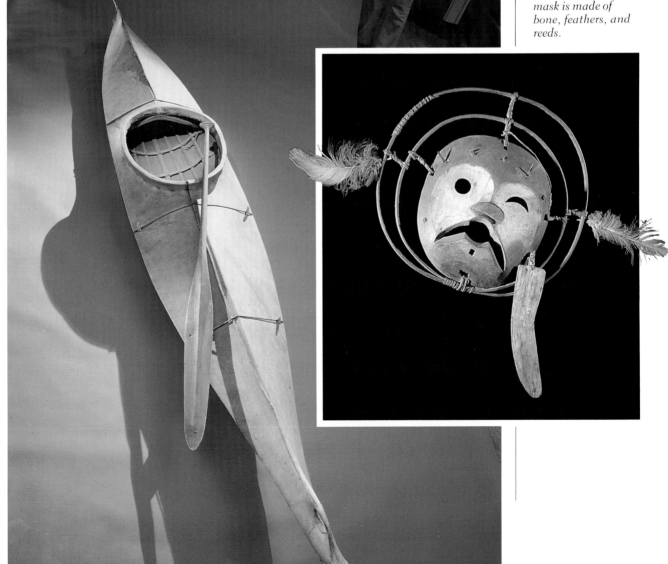

apart from all other languages. It varied little from one Eskimo region of the far north to another.

Because their environment was such a difficult one in which to live, the Eskimos paid extremely close attention to it. They were aware of small differences that people from lands farther south would probably not even notice, and they used very precise expressions to describe them.

Thus, the Eskimo language contains more than 30 different words for snow. Old snow on the ground is *aputiqarniq*, while new snow on the ground is *qaniktaq*. Snow with a hard crust on top is *qirsuqaktuq*, but soft snow that you sink into is *mauja*. There are at least 15 words for different kinds of wind, and for different kinds of ice as well. Even an animal is called by different names depending on whether you see it on an ice raft, a rock, or a sandy coastal plain.

Ancient Artifacts. The oldest evidence—so far—of human habitation south of Alaska has been found in what is today the state of New Mexico. One group of spearpoints and ancient animal bones was found near Clovis, N.M. These points, now some 11,500 years old, measure from 2.5 to 4.5 inches (6.2 to 12.2 centimeters) long.

The other find was discovered near Folsom, N.M., and dates to about 10,500 years ago. An African-American cowboy named George McJunken found the first Folsom point in the early 1920's. It is long, thin, and fluted. That is, a narrow flake had been removed down the center of the point's faces. After McJunken's initial find, Folsom points were also uncovered in what is now Colorado and Wyoming.

Folsom points were the first evidence that human beings lived in North America during the Ice Age. Before McJunken's discovery, most scientists believed that the first people came to North America much more recently.

INDIANS OF NORTH AMERICA

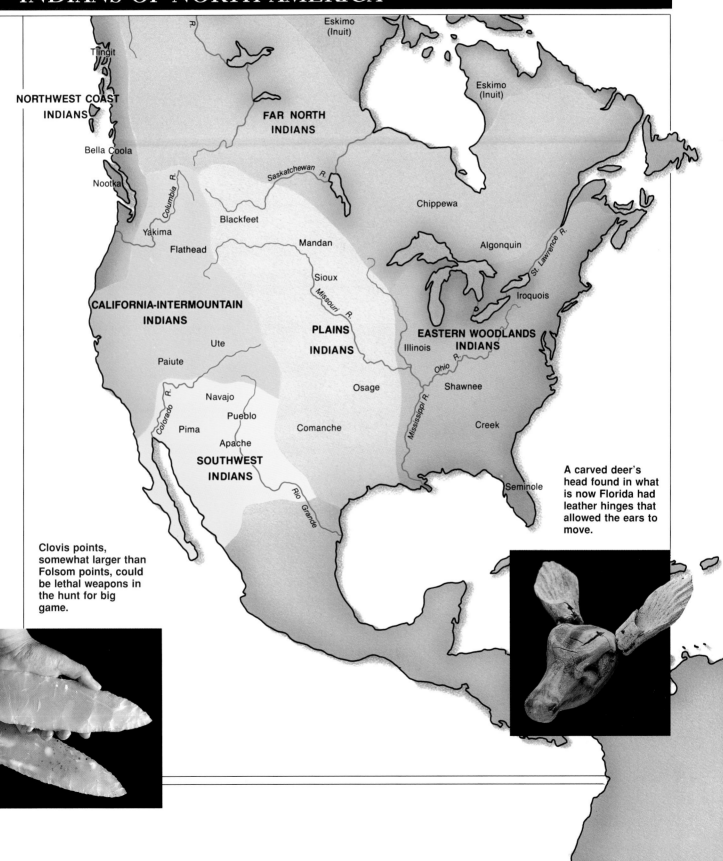

Eskimo
(Inuit)

Yukon R.

Eskimo
(Inuit)

Tlingit

Eskimo
(Inuit)

NORTHWEST COAST
INDIANS

FAR NORTH
INDIANS

Bella Coola

Nootka

Columbia R.

Saskatchewan R.

Chippewa

Blackfeet

Yakima

Flathead

Mandan

Algonquin

St. Lawrence R.

Sioux

Iroquois

Missouri R.

CALIFORNIA-INTERMOUNTAIN
INDIANS

PLAINS
INDIANS

EASTERN WOODLANDS
INDIANS

Ute

Illinois

Paiute

Osage

Ohio R.

Shawnee

Colorado R.

Navajo

Pueblo

Pima

Comanche

Creek

Apache

Mississippi R.

SOUTHWEST
INDIANS

Rio Grande

Seminole

A carved deer's
head found in what
is now Florida had
leather hinges that
allowed the ears to
move.

Clovis points,
somewhat larger than
Folsom points, could
be lethal weapons in
the hunt for big
game.

The Northwest Coast. What are now classified as Indians of the Northwest Coast included those in present-day Alaska, Canada, Oregon, and Washington. Among the tribes were Tlingit, Haida, Bella Coola, and Nootka. Groups in Washington and Oregon lived in an environment of abundance. The rivers and ocean were thick with fish—salmon, cod, herring, and halibut. Forested areas of the coastal region offered a great variety of nuts, berries, and small game for food. Indians used the abundant fir and redwood trees to build houses and to make clothes and bedding.

During spring and summer, many Indians could hunt and gather enough food to last throughout the year. Fall and winter were given over to festivals and ceremonies, for the weaving of blankets and baskets, and for woodcarving. The Haida and Kwakiutl in particular were known for their fine woodcarving.

Totem poles were common in the Northwest. These were clan or tribal emblems and other symbols carved in the trunk of a tree that had been felled just for the purpose. The carvings usually depicted the animal, bird, or fish associated with the clan or tribe. Among some groups, a totem pole had religious significance. Among others, it was merely a tribal or clan expression. A tribe usually held a ceremonial feast called a potlatch after a totem pole had been completed.

The term *potlatch* comes from the Nootka word *patshatl*, meaning *giving*. The ceremony offered a person, usually a chief, an opportunity to show off wealth—not by simply displaying and bragging about possessions, but by giving them away. All the food provided for the potlatch had to be eaten before the festivities ended. A potlatch also involved giving away items such as finely woven blankets, cedar chests, and sea otter skins. The feasts were held in special buildings called potlatch houses, which featured elaborate wood carvings on the outside. The potlatch ceremonies caused great rivalries between the various chiefs and clan leaders. Whoever gave the next potlatch had to make it more lavish and expansive than the last.

The California-Intermountain Groups. More than 200 different tribes lived in what is now the large area including California as well as parts of Nevada, Utah, Idaho, Washington, Oregon, Montana, and Colorado. The tribes included Yakima, Flathead, Nez Perce, Shoshone, Modoc, Ute, Paiute, and Mohave.

Nearly all of these Indians lived by hunting and gathering. They made a variety of dishes from acorn flour, hunted small game and birds, and gathered berries. Like the Indians of the Northwest Coast, those of the California-Intermountain region lived in a land of abundance.

The Southwest. Although the Clovis and Folsom spearpoints indicated that people lived in the Southwest about 10,000 years ago, little is known about these ancient immigrants. It is an environment where rainfall is sparse and game and edible wild plants were hard to find. One group that did succeed, though, are called the Hohokam, a group who are believed to be the ancestors of the Pima. Living in the area near present-day Phoenix, Az., the Hohokam people built dams and dug ditches to channel water from nearby rivers to their fields. With this water supply, the Hohokam grew several things, but corn was their main crop. Traces of Hohokam irrigation ditches show that some of them were 25 feet (7.5 meters) wide and 15 feet (4.5 meters) deep. One network of ditches along the Salt River was about 150 miles (240 kilometers) long.

The people known now as cliff dwellers actually represented several tribes, including the Hopi and the Zuñi. They flourished in the Southwest between A.D. 1000 and 1300. The cliff dwellers grew corn and other crops, and they hunted game to supplement their grain and vegetable diets. They created beautiful pottery and used the fibers of yucca and milkweed plants, along with cotton, to weave cloth.

The cliff dwellers got their name from their unusual adobe brick buildings that extended two, three, or sometimes more stories up the faces of steep cliffs or below cliff overhangs. These homes had few entrances on the first level. People used ladders, which they drew up behind them, or steps cut into the nearby rock to enter their unusual dwellings at the second or third levels. Circular rooms called *kivas* were entered through holes in the roofs by ladders. Kivas were used for meetings of tribal councils and as sites for religious ceremonies. Kiva walls were plastered and richly painted in yellow, green, white, and red. However, these ornate buildings

A totem pole (as shown opposite) was often brightly painted by its makers. However, exposure to the elements frequently faded many of those that still exist.

A restored kiva in Cliff Palace at Mesa Verde National Park. The wooden ladder and ceiling are modern recreations.

With its 200 rooms and 23 kivas, the spectacular Cliff Palace is just one of dozens of pueblos found at Mesa Verde National Park. Others include Spruce Tree House with 120 rooms and Long House with 150.

were the domain of men only; women were forbidden to enter.

The Anasazi, meaning the "ancient ones," began developing multi-storied shelters around A.D. 1000, and are among the best-known cliff dwellers. The largest Anasazi village, called Cliff Palace, housed more than 400 people and is today part of Mesa Verde National Park, in southwestern Colorado. About A.D. 1300, the Anasazi abandoned Cliff Palace, probably due to a severe drought that had lasted almost a quarter of a century. It is believed they headed southeast in search of water, probably at the Rio Grande, and became the ancestors of the Hopi and the Zuñi.

The Hopi and the Zuñi were two of the groups that were later named Pueblo Indians by Spanish explorers. *Pueblo* is the Spanish word for village. Pueblo Indians lived in New Mexico, Arizona, southern Colorado, and Utah. Pueblo culture was largely governed by tribal religious leaders. As part of their religious celebrations, Pueblo men performed *kachina* dances in which they wore masks that symbolized the spirits of water, earth, and sky. Pueblo Indians made excellent pottery, beautiful baskets, cotton cloth, and blankets. Hopi, Zuñi, and other Pueblo groups still live in the southwestern United States today.

Migrants to the Southwest. The Apaches were later arrivals to the Southwest, as were the Navajo, a tribe that split off from the original

Kachina dolls were not playthings but rather objects to be treasured and studied by their young owners to learn about the many different supernatural beings that the dolls represented. These included Ahote, a singer of sacred songs, and Narashka, who disciplined erring children. Today, such dolls are collectors' items.

Apaches. These groups began migrating to the Southwest from northern Canada about A.D. 1000.

The Navajos and the Apaches were farmers whose crops supplied most of their food. Their masterful irrigation systems made farming possible in the relatively dry Southwest. However, like other Indians of the Southwest, they also gathered and ate prickly pears, yucca, and sunflower seeds.

The Plains Indians.

The Great Plains extend from what is now northern Canada south to Texas and from the Rocky Mountains east to present-day South Dakota, Nebraska, Kansas, and Oklahoma. The earliest Indians on the Great Plains may have been hunters from forested areas near the Mississippi who hunted buffalo periodically in the short-grass region. At that time, there were no horses in North America. An earlier small horse had become extinct. Buffalo hunters had to journey to and from the Plains and hunt prey entirely on foot.

To approach a North American bison, or "buffalo," individual hunters often covered themselves with a buffalo skin and crept slowly and patiently to within shooting distance, trying not to frighten the nervous herd. The hunters hoped to bring an animal down with a single arrow shot from a bow. If the terrain permitted, hunters worked together to stampede a buffalo herd over a nearby cliff.

At the bottom, they finished off wounded animals with arrows and spears and skinned the carcasses with stone knives. Hunters then lashed the meat and hides to two long poles to make a type of sled. Teams of dogs pulled the sled back to the villages. When Spanish explorers brought the first horses to the Southwest in the 1500's, buffalo hunting and other aspects of Indian life were forever changed. Horses made buffalo hunting much easier. Thus Indians such as the Sioux, Blackfeet, Cheyenne, and Pawnee were able to take up permanent life on the Plains.

Most Plains Indians were nomadic. They followed the migrating buffalo herds, and their ways of life came to depend almost entirely on those shaggy, bearded creatures.

The Indians used the buffalo to fulfill a variety of needs. They used buffalo as a major source of food, especially the meat, but also internal organs, bone marrow, and blood as well. They fashioned clothing from buffalo hides, including warm robes that protected them against the Great Plains' wintry blasts. Hides were also a major component of the Indian homes called tepees. Hides were stretched across the long poles that formed a tepee frame. Indians also made shields and saddles from buffalo

Because they were used to wolves, buffalo herds often took no notice when hunters disguised in wolfskins crept within bowshot. This portion of a painting by well-known artist George Catlin is a good illustration of the tactic.

hides, and they used buffalo bladders as water bags. Sometimes, Indians stuffed the hides with buffalo hair to make a ball used in various games. Buffalo bones were carved into tools, and the animal's sinews served as strings and backing for bows. Horns were fashioned into spoons, cups, or bowls. Tails became fly swatters or whips. Buffalo "chips," or manure, served as fuel.

The Mandans living along the Missouri River were an exception to the nomadic lifestyle of many other Great Plains groups. The Mandans lived in permanent villages of circular earthen lodges made with frames of cottonwood logs covered with brush and soil. They were mainly farmers, and their major crop was corn. However, they did venture out into the Missouri River in small, round boats known as *bullboats*. These were made by constructing a frame of bent willow branches and covering it with buffalo hide. However, the circular shape made the bullboats difficult to maneuver.

The Woodland Indians. Some groups now known as Woodland Indians settled between the Mississippi River and the Atlantic Ocean. Inter-

laced with streams and dotted with lakes, the area was thick with hardwood forests in the north and huge pine forests in the south.

The earliest Woodland cultures date back 9,000 years to a period now known as Eastern Archaic. One Archaic site has been discovered along the Illinois side of the Mississippi River southeast of St. Louis. It became known as the Modoc Rock Shelter. Layers of artifacts unearthed there by archaeologists revealed that several different peoples occupied the site over a long period. The earliest groups apparently hunted deer, opossum, raccoon, and elk, and fished for slow-moving catfish in the backwaters of the Mississippi. Later artifacts suggest that people eventually added plant foods and migrant fowl to their diets and that they had domesticated dogs.

Two early Woodland cultures were those now called the Adena and Hopewell. They are known for their construction of huge burial mounds. The Adena culture began to build large mounds about 700 B.C. The culture was spread across what is now Indiana, Ohio, northern Kentucky, northwestern West Virginia, and Pennsylvania. The Adena people built burial mounds that served as graves for chiefs and other important people. Over time, several layers of burials increased the height of the mounds, with one rising about 70 feet (21 meters) aboveground. Complexes of mounds were surrounded by earthen walls that measured about 500 feet (150 meters) in diameter. The Adena buried personal items, such as jewelry, along with the bodies.

The Hopewell people were named after the owner of a farm in central Ohio where more than 30 mounds were found. The Hopewell people and their culture flourished from about 100 B.C. to A.D. 500. They also lived in what is now Illinois, Indiana, Iowa, and Wisconsin.

Many of the Hopewell mounds were effigies — representations of liv-

ing creatures—and may have had religious significance. The most elaborate effigy is the Great Serpent Mound in Ohio.

Most of the Hopewell dead were cremated. The burial of the body seems to have been reserved for an upper class, probably made up of chiefs and other important people.

Much of what is known about the Hopewell people comes from examining the contents of excavated mounds. Evidence of their familiarity with corn has been found, for example. Also there is strong evidence that the Hopewell people were traders who came into contact with other groups from a large geographic area. Copper ore for objects in the mounds probably came from Indians of the Great Lakes region. Shells, along with shark and alligator teeth, probably origi-

Four Bears, the last of the great Mandan chiefs, was a noted warrior, negotiator, and religious leader. In this portrait by George Catlin, Four Bears's quilled shirt adorned with locks of hair and his warbonnet bespeak his prowess as a great military leader.

Great Serpent Mound is one of six major Hopewell sites that have been excavated in Ohio. Many scholars believe that there may be more than a hundred others.

nated in the Gulf of Mexico region. Stone for pipes may have come from Minnesota and Wisconsin. Obsidian and grizzly bear teeth were probably brought by Indian traders from the Rocky Mountains.

After about 400, Hopewellian mounds became less elaborate and carefully fashioned. About A.D. 500, the Hopewell trade network collapsed and the people themselves faded from the scene.

However, beginning about A.D. 700, another mound-building people developed along the Mississippi River, from what is now Illinois south to the state of Mississippi. These people built tall earthen pyramids topped by wooden temples, earning them the name *temple builders*. The temple mound at Cahokia, Ill., south of St. Louis, is the largest of these.

The Iroquois. The Iroquois, who lived mainly in the northern part of what is now New York state, were Woodland Indians. Divided into the Five Nations — the Oneida, Cayuga, Mohawk, Onondaga, and Seneca —

the Iroquois referred to themselves as *Ongwanonhsioni*, which means *we long house builders*. The Iroquois lived in long houses made of saplings covered with bark and sometimes measuring about 100 feet (30 meters) long and 30 feet (9 meters) wide. *Palisades*, or tall staked fences, often surrounded their villages as protection.

Like other Woodland Indians, the Iroquois were farmers as well as hunters and gatherers. The "Three Sisters" of the Iroquois were corn, beans, and squash. Using fire and tools such as stone axes, the men cleared patches of forest for use as farm fields. The women planted, tended, and harvested the crops.

The women let their black hair grow long and tied it so that it hung down their backs. The men had a streak of hair about two fingers long and three fingers wide running from the forehead across the top of the head to the neck. They cut the hair on either side of the streak close to the scalp, except for a long lock they left dangling from one side of the head. Today, such a hairstyle — with or without the long lock — is often called a Mohawk.

The Iroquois were known as fierce fighters by their neighbors. "They approach like foxes, fight like angry lions, and fly away like birds," according to one who knew them well. However, they fought each other about as often as they fought outside enemies until, according to Iroquois legend, Dekanawidah and Hiawatha developed their plan for the Great League.

According to legend, Dekanawidah was a Huron from north of the St. Lawrence River who traveled south to live with the Mohawk. He wished to sit with tribal leaders beneath the great world-tree and seal eternal peace. However no one listened to Dekanawidah until Hiawatha, a Mohawk, heard of him and his message of peace. Together, he and Hiawatha worked out the details of the Great League and then set out to persuade members of the Five Nations to accept their plan. The Mohawk were the first to agree; then the remaining four nations fell into line.

A council of 50 *sachems*, or chiefs, presided over the Great League of the Iroquois. The women of each tribe selected the sachems.

Even though each sachem was supposed to serve a lifelong term, the women could remove those whom they believed had not fulfilled their duties properly.

The Great League benefited the Iroquois in both peace and war. It brought peace to the Five Nations themselves, and also it enabled them to act in concert against their enemies, which increased Iroquois power and influence among their neighbors.

Farther south lived groups such as the Tuscarora, Creek, Chickasaw, Cherokee, and Choctaw. *Creek* was actually a name given to any of 19 tribes living in what are now the states of Alabama and Georgia. Several of these peoples, including the Alabama and Muskogee, belonged to the loosely organized Creek Confederacy. By the time they met the first European explorers in the year 1540, the Creeks lived in about 50 villages, some of which had more than a thousand inhabitants. Although basically made up of tribes of farmers, the Creek Confederacy grew in military importance during colonial times as it expanded to include additional tribes displaced by European settlers.

Virtually all Iroquois Indians lived in long houses. When two people married, the groom came to live in the long house of the bride. Inside a long house, each family had a booth that could be curtained off for privacy.

About A.D. 700, a Native American culture began to develop in what are now the southern and Mississippi Valley regions of the United States. Characteristic of the *Mississippian cul-*

MISSISSIPPIAN CULTURE

ture, as this civilization came to be known, were large, flat-topped monuments of earth, often called *temple mounds*, built as platforms for temples and official residences. The Mississippian peoples lived in cities, some of which grew to great size. The largest was Cahokia, in present-day Illinois.

Sprawled on the east bank of the Mississippi River and surrounded by fields of corn, beans, and squash, Cahokia was a bustling trade center and home to about 40,000 merchants, artisans, laborers, farmers, and hunter-gatherers. They lived in sim-

ple, rectangular huts built of logs placed upright in the earth and topped with thatch. City life centered around a main plaza containing the temple mound. The people's huts were arranged in rows around the plaza.

Traders from near and far came to Cahokia to exchange valuable raw materials for arrowheads, leather goods, pottery, jewelry, and ceremonial items made by Cahokian craftworkers. From nearby settlements, traders brought a type of rock called

chert, favored by Cahokian artisans for fashioning into arrowheads and blades for farming tools. Other traders brought exotic materials used by Cahokian jewelry makers: copper from the north, grizzly bear teeth and claws from distant western regions, and pastel shells and shimmering pearls from the southern sea now known as the Gulf of Mexico.

Cahokia had a complex government headed by a ruler-priest, who conducted religious ceremonies and, along with lesser priests, formed the town's ruling aristocracy. In addition to their religious and governmental

duties, priests were responsible for overseeing communal storehouses filled with corn, game, and other foods.

As the leaders of Cahokian spiritual and political life, priests lived in luxury. Servants prepared their meals and carried them through the streets on high couches called *litters* so that their feet would not touch the ground.

Archaeological evidence suggests that when a priest died, the people of Cahokia sacrificed his servants so they could attend to his needs in the afterlife. A priest's burial mound excavated in the 1960's contained the remains of four men whose heads

This painting shows what scholars think Cahokia may have looked like about A.D. 1150.

This bird statue was found at Cahokia. The figure is made of hammered copper.

Today, visitors to Cahokia can climb on some of the mounds. Steps have been installed to make the climbing easier.

and hands had been cut off and more than 50 young women.

Cahokia's temple mound was the largest in what is now the United States. Today, it is called Monk's Mound because a community of Trappist monks lived nearby during the 1800's. The mound towers 100 feet (30 meters), and its base is bigger than that of the Great Pyramid in Egypt. Construction of the mound was begun about A.D. 900 and completed about 1150. It may have honored the sun, a deity.

Other sites of Mississippian culture with similar temple mounds have been found in Oklahoma, Alabama, Georgia, and Mississippi. The civilization flourished until the 1500's, when diseases brought by Europeans, such as smallpox, measles, and tuberculosis, killed many of the people.

Only one Mississippian group, the Natchez Indians, survived long enough to be fully described by Europeans. Their city was called Natchez, near the present-day city of Natchez, Miss. In 1729, the French governor of the region ordered the Natchez people to leave their main village because he wanted to develop a plantation there. Furious, the Natchez rose up in revolt and killed 200 French immigrants. The French in turn slaughtered most of the Natchez, burned some at the stake, and sold the rest into slavery in the Caribbean. Mississippian culture had come to an end.

The Inca Indians of South America made wonderful roads, some of which are still in use. This Inca road runs from Lake Titicaca into the nearby mountains. A Chimu artisan, who lived in South America before the Inca, made the gold ceremonial gloves shown here.

CHAPTER 3: GROUPS OF THE CARIBBEAN, CENTRAL, AND SOUTH AMERICA

Indians of the Caribbean lived in the southern half of Central America, the northern parts of present-day Venezuela and Colombia, and on the Caribbean islands. This region was tropical, but the climate was pleasant owing to high altitudes or breezes from the sea.

Arawak Indians lived in the coastal areas. Arawaks who lived on the islands called themselves *Tainos*. Other tribes included the Lenca and Cuna of Central America and the Chibcha of Colombia.

The Olmec Indians of Central America are well known today for the gigantic carved stone heads they made. Some of these heads weigh as much as 36,000 pounds (16,300 kilograms) each.

Indians of the Caribbean grew a variety of food crops, including avocados, beans, corn, peanuts, peppers, pineapples, and sweet potatoes. Most of these Indians wore clothing made of cotton, a native plant. They made pottery, and they used gold and copper to create ornaments and tools. Most Caribbean Indians lived in villages of thatched houses often surrounded by palisades. The center of the community was the house of the chief, or king, and the temples.

Warfare played an important part in the lives of many Caribbean Indians, and they used weapons such as slings, spear throwers, clubs, and blowguns. Some also used bows and arrows. The Tainos, however, were an exception. Violence played an exceedingly minor role in their society. The Tainos were warm, friendly, and generous, as reported by Christopher Columbus himself. He noted that the Tainos of the island he named Hispaniola:

are very unskilled in arms. . . . In all the world there is no better people nor better country. They love their neighbors as themselves, and they have the sweetest talk in the world, and are gentle and are always laughing.

Middle America.
Indians migrating south from the Bering Strait reached what is now Mexico about 8000 B.C. Within a thousand years they had developed farming, making permanent villages possible. Many groups, including the Olmec, Maya, Toltec, and Aztec, created great civilizations with magnificent cities.

ducted religious ceremonies honoring the sun, rain, and corn gods, as well as the moon goddess, and other deities.

Mayan cities also contained ball courts where athletes played Pok-ta-Pok, a game resembling a combination of modern-day basketball and soccer. The ball court measured 75 feet (22.5 meters) long by 25 feet (7.6 meters) wide and had sloping walls on either side. There were two teams of up to 11 players each. The object of the game was to hit a small, hard rubber ball using only shoulders, elbows, or hips. When the game was first played, athletes had to hit the ball against a side marker or else send it into the opposing team's end zone. After a while, however, that seemed too easy, so the Maya changed the

At. . .The Observatory priests watched and recorded the movements of the sun, moon, and planets.

The Olmecs, whose civilization flourished between 1200 and 200 B.C. in modern-day Mexico, left many artifacts behind that continue to puzzle archaeologists. Among these are huge stone humanlike heads topped with coverings resembling helmets. Some of these heads stand 8 feet (2.4 meters) high and weigh 40 tons (36 metric tons). Half-human, half-jaguar figures, frequently carved from jade and perhaps representing a god, appear in various Olmec arts. The Olmecs may have developed an elementary form of hieroglyphic writing. Their major city was La Venta.

Sometime after the Olmecs, the Maya built large cities in what is now Guatemala, and on the Yucatán Peninsula. Dominated by huge stone pyramids with temples on top, these cities may have been primarily religious centers. From these, priests con-

rules. Now a player had to direct the ball through a stone hoop that was fastened sideways on either sidewall 25 feet (7.6 meters) high above the playing ground.

Playing Pok-ta-Pok called for great skill and agility. Athletes protected themselves by wearing special leather equipment, including a helmet, a wide belt, and pads for the knees and hips.

Although Pok-ta-Pok began as a sport, it eventually turned into a religious ritual. The ball became a symbol of the sun, while the game itself became a symbol of the struggle between life and death. As a consequence, members of the losing team were sacrificed.

Remarkable achievements in art and science characterized Mayan civilization. The Maya created outstanding painting, pottery, and architec-

ture. At cities such as Chichén Itzá in the Yucatán Peninsula, the Maya built some of the largest pyramids in the world. Archaeologists believe that the "great pyramid" in the city had a scientific as well as a religious function. At one major building now called The Observatory, priests watched and recorded the movements of the sun, moon, and planets. Observers kept records in a type of hieroglyphic writing on stone slabs called stelae. From their observations,

Mayan priests developed two calendars. One calendar of 260 days served religious purposes. The other, a nearly perfect 365-day calendar, was used to determine planting seasons and other facets of daily life.

Mayan civilization reached its peak around A.D. 250 and continued to flourish for another 600 years. Then it collapsed. Crop failure, disease, armed invasion, or perhaps a combination of all three, may have been responsible.

The Observatory at Chichén Itzá is just one of the attractions that draws thousands of tourists annually. Chichén Itzá was an important religious site as well as a political capital, and its sacred well received human sacrifices along with offerings of jade, pottery, gold, cloth, and wood.

The pyramids at Chichén Itzá are among the tallest in the world. This one was called El Castillo by the Spanish conquerors, and it retains that name today. The huge carved Toltec warrior-column at Tula is just one of several still standing there.

A group called the Toltecs from the central Mexican highlands eventually took over the Yucatán Peninsula and ruled there until about the year 1200.

The Toltecs originated in northern Mexico and reached the central highlands about 900. Tula, located 60 miles (96.5 kilometers) north of present-day Mexico City, was their major city. There Toltecs erected pyramid-temples, the main structure being dedicated to Quetzalcóatl, the Plumed Serpent, who, according to Toltec legend, founded Tula. Great stone columns in the form of animal and human figures supported the roof of Quetzalcóatl's temple. They remain as part of Toltec ruins today.

The Toltecs were the precursors of the Aztecs, who also worshipped Quetzalcóatl and who became the most powerful people of ancient Mexico. Like the Toltecs, the Aztecs migrated from northern Mexico to the central highlands. They arrived sometime in the 1200's.

At that time, people far more civilized than the Aztecs dominated the region, residing in such cities as Texcoco, Tenayuca, Tepeycac, and Culhuancan. They did not welcome the newcomers, whom they regarded as arrogant, bellicose, and deceitful.

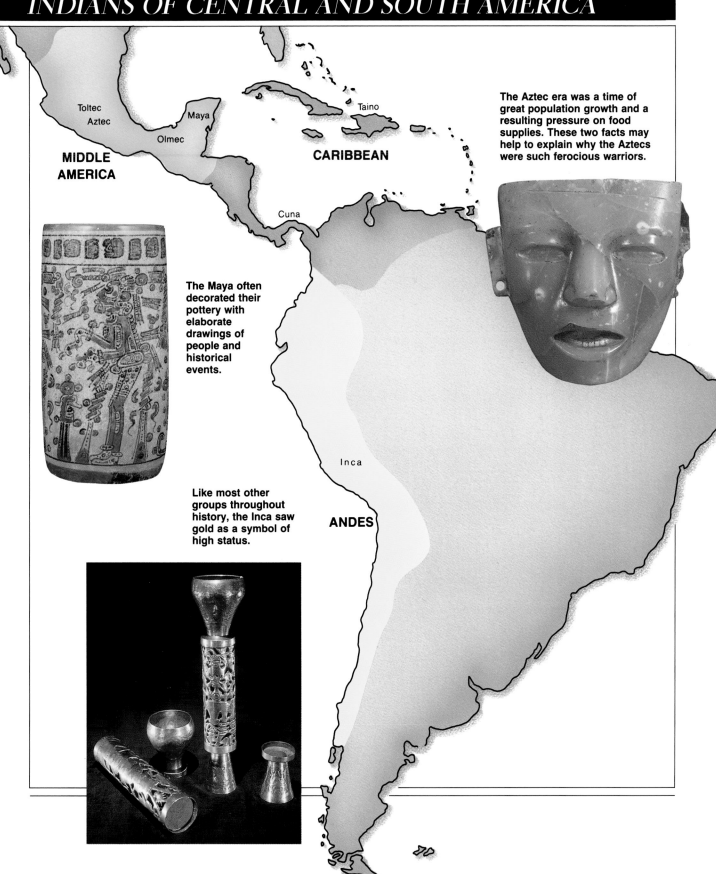

INDIANS OF CENTRAL AND SOUTH AMERICA

Toltec
Aztec
Olmec
Maya

**MIDDLE
AMERICA**

Taino

CARIBBEAN

Cuna

The Aztec era was a time of great population growth and a resulting pressure on food supplies. These two facts may help to explain why the Aztecs were such ferocious warriors.

The Maya often decorated their pottery with elaborate drawings of people and historical events.

Inca

ANDES

Like most other groups throughout history, the Inca saw gold as a symbol of high status.

The Aztecs were an aggressive people who seemed to regard themselves as destined to rule. They settled on the hill of Chapultepec, now a park in Mexico City, only to be driven from there to a barren island near the western shore of Lake Texcoco.

The Aztecs proved to be highly skilled builders on their island. There they built Tenochtitlan, their great city of 100,000 people. Canals as well as wide, straight streets provided transportation routes. Magnificent temples and well-cared-for homes lined the streets. Each day, a small army of workers kept the streets and buildings clean. Floating gardens supplied the people with much of their food. Causeways that could be closed at the threat of invasion—simplifying the problem of defense—connected Tenochtitlan with the mainland.

Tenochtitlan had schools that all Aztec children were required to attend, hosts of shops where artisans of all sorts labored, and academies for training priests. Many priests were needed, because religion played a vital role in Aztec life—thousands of priests served the main temple of Tenochtitlan alone. This immense pyramid-temple, like others the Aztecs built, was similar to those the Maya and other groups of Middle America had erected.

Aztec artisans made striking mosaics from the feathers of the quetzal and other birds. Artisans also fashioned unusually attractive gold and silver jewelry. Lapidarists turned out fine jewelry and mosaics from jadeite, turquoise, and other precious stones. These artists and others such as composers and poets held places of honor in Aztec society.

The Aztecs developed a permanent, formal government, with a hierarchy consisting of a king, nobles, priests, bureaucrats, and common people. The king and his council of nobles made and administered laws. The bureaucrats helped with the administration and were responsible for such things as running the schools, maintaining the streets and canals, and keeping Tenochtitlan clean.

The Aztecs were superb soldiers. Toward the end of the 1300's they began to expand their territory, and they soon conquered most of the peoples of the highland areas and southern Mexico. They established a great empire,

The Aztec Calendar Stone is 12 feet (3.7 meters) in diameter. It was used in ceremonies honoring the sun god Tonatiuh, whose face is in the center. The Calendar Stone is the most famous surviving piece of Aztec sculpture, and it is on exhibit at the Museum of Anthropological History in Mexico City.

and their king became a mighty emperor with many subjects.

However the Aztecs did not wage war in order to gain territory or to force their way of life on others. Instead, they used warfare as a way to gain tribute, which might consist of cotton cloth, precious stones, jaguar skins, food, or dyes. At the same time, warfare was also a way to ensure a steady supply of the human sacrifices the Aztecs needed for their religious rituals. The Aztecs believed that their existence as a people depended on keeping in the good graces of their gods. The only way to do that they believed was to regularly offer up the "human liquid" they thought their gods demanded. Priests slashed open the chest of a living victim and tore out the heart. On some occasions, hundreds of people were sacrificed in a single day. The Aztecs were not the only Amerindians to practice human sacrifice. They did so, however, with greater regularity and diligence than any other group.

The Andes. By the 1400's, the Aztec empire reached its peak. However, the Inca empire of South America was just beginning. The word *Inca* originally meant *king*, or *ruler*, and he was called the *Sapa Inca* (Only King). The word *Inca* later came to mean the people themselves.

According to legend, the Incas originally lived along the shores of clear, icy Lake Titicaca, on the border between what are now Bolivia and Peru. About A.D. 1200, the Incas obeyed the command of their Sun God and migrated northwest. They finally settled in a high valley in the Andes Mountains, where they built the city of Cusco.

The legend goes on to explain how the Incas knew where to build their city. Manco Capac, the Inca leader and a son of the Sun God, had received a golden staff from his father. As he and his followers moved from place to place, Manco Capac would

The huge Pyramid of the Sun now stands in mute testimony to the grandeur of the former city of Teotihuacan, which was deliberately destroyed about A.D. 750. Today, no one knows exactly why this happened, but it paved the way for the rise of the Aztecs and their god-king, Quetzalcoatl.

The imposing Inca city of Machu Picchu covers more than 100 acres (40 hectares) of steep terrain high in the Andes. Its fine granite buildings included a fortress, public baths, temples, individual homes, and a royal palace. The gold dagger was made by the Chimu people, who lived in South America about A.D. 1000.

thrust the staff into the ground. Each time the staff barely penetrated before hitting rock. Finally in the valley of Cusco, Manco Capac's staff went all the way in. Now he knew that the soil was deep and fertile and that the valley was a good place in which to settle.

About 1438, during the reign of Pachacuti, the ninth Sapa Inca, the Incas began to bring neighboring groups under their control. The empire reached its zenith about a hundred years later during the reign of Huayna Capac, who unified the conquered regions of present-day Ecuador and Colombia. The Incas then ruled about 12 million people.

Well-built roads served to connect Cusco with other Inca cities such as Quito in the north and Tumbes on the Pacific coast. These magnificent highways were about 20 feet (6 meters) wide and had solved numerous building problems caused by the steep terrain. On unusually steep slopes, the road became steps chiseled out of rock. Deep gorges were spanned with bridges of thick rope.

No wheeled vehicles used the roads. The Incas, like other Native Americans, did not use the wheel for transportation. Traffic consisted of humans traveling on foot and llamas, which were used as pack animals. The

the government and was aided by a brother or uncle who served as chief priest, conducting numerous religious ceremonies, such as those concerning the planting season and the harvest. A council of nobles, made up largely of other members of the Sapa Inca's family, acted as the emperor's advisers.

Inca weavers produced fine woolen cloth decorated with elaborate geometric designs. Artisans who worked with gold turned out figurines of animals and humans, as well as drinking goblets and fine jewelry. Inca builders are especially remembered for the fine technical quality of their temples and other buildings. Constructed of blocks of stone, these buildings were so well designed that the stone blocks fit together perfectly without the use of mortar. The Temple to the Sun in Cusco, a stone edifice covered with sheets of gold, was especially magnificent. Inside, gold and silver lined the walls, and in the main room, a great golden likeness of the Sun covered an entire wall. Another room, which belonged to the Moon, the bride of the Sun, had lovely silver-covered walls and contained a silver symbol of the Moon.

An excellent example of Inca stonework can be seen today at the ruins of Machu Picchu. This great fortress-city stands high in the Andes Mountains overlooking the Grand Canyon of the Urubamba River in Peru. The mountain fortress is believed to have been the last hiding place of the Inca nobles who fled from the Spanish conquerors in the 1500's. No one today knows how long the Inca nobles or their descendants may have remained there, but eventually the city was abandoned. The ruins of Machu Picchu were "discovered" in 1911 by archaeologist Hiram Bingham.

The Inca empire, like the Aztec, was doomed. By the 1530's, both empires lay in ruins, a consequence of the appearance of the next immigrants to the Americas — the Spanish.

roads were particularly useful for quickly moving the huge Inca army from one part of the empire to another.

Like the Aztecs, the Incas did not impose their way of life on conquered peoples, leaving them alone so long as they paid tribute. Tribute in the Inca empire consisted of food, work on public projects such as building roads or mining gold and silver, and service in the Inca army.

Also like the Aztecs, the Incas had a formal government with a very well-organized bureaucracy that collected tribute and oversaw road building and maintenance. The emperor headed

PART 2: THE EUROPEANS ARRIVE

This painting from about 1521 shows the sturdy, three-masted ships called carracks that were used by early explorers. The high stern areas provided living quarters for the captain and other officers.

In the early 1300's, a great cultural movement called the *Renaissance* began in Europe. This magnificent time of human existence was the era of da Vinci, Michelangelo, Shakespeare, and Lorenzo de Medici. People turned away from the beliefs of the past and broke the intellectual chains that had held them. It is no accident that the great voyages of discovery took place also. In a sense, Columbus' voyage in 1492 was one of the greatest achievements of the era.

Early maps were often part fact and part fancy. However, knowledge improved with each voyage. Astrolabes, such as the one above, helped navigators make these journeys. Rulers, such as Ferdinand and Isabella, often funded the trips.

CHAPTER 4: COLUMBUS AND THOSE BEFORE HIM

By the 1400's, traders and fishers were venturing out from the small nation of Portugal into the Atlantic Ocean. By this time, the Portuguese had already mastered the seafaring technology that made long ocean voyages possible, and they led all European nations in voyages beyond the horizon. Soon, others, especially the Spanish, were becoming avid explorers, too.

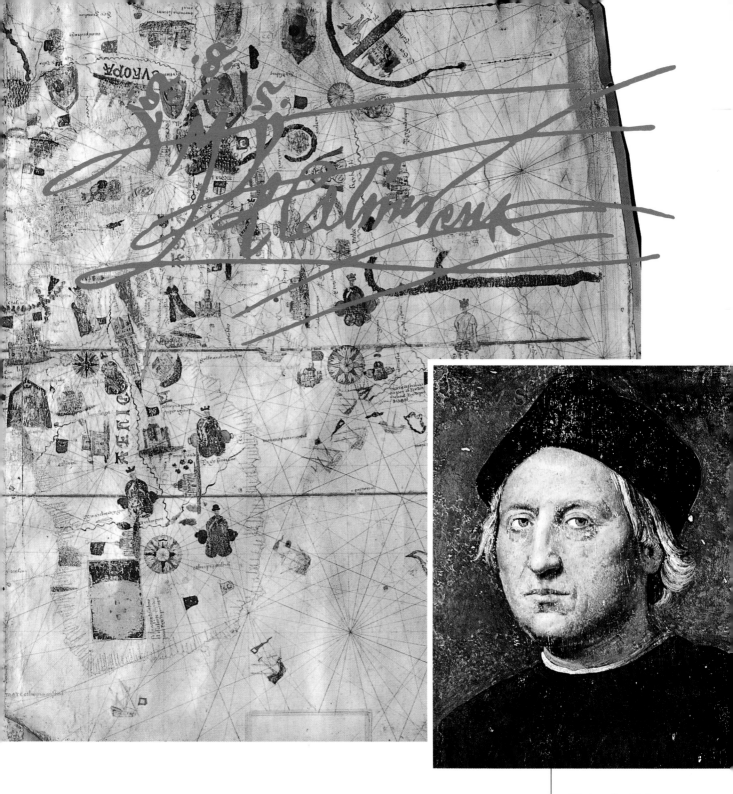

Scholars and historians disagree about exactly who the first European arrivals were and when they reached the Americas. However, most agree that Eric the Red, a Norwegian Viking who had been living in Iceland, sailed with his family to Greenland about A.D. 982. It is believed now that plague and disease in Europe is what prompted Eric and others to go. Then, in about 10 years, all the good cropland in Greenland had been taken. Interest soon rose in traveling to a land that had been sighted farther west when a ship sailing from Iceland to Greenland had gone off course.

About 1000, Leif Ericson, a son of Eric the Red, led an expedition to the

Christopher Columbus late in his life as painted by Ridolfo del Ghirlandaio. After 1492, Columbus began signing himself "Al Almirante" to signify his title of Admiral of the Ocean Sea.

new territory. He and his crew landed somewhere on the east coast of North America and spent the winter there. They made wine from the plentiful supply of grapes they found, and Ericson called the area *Vinland* (Wineland.) The Vikings soon established a colony in Vinland, but in time they were driven away by the Indians and did not return.

In their battles, both the Vikings and the Indians used weapons that surprised and terrified the other side, which had never seen them before.

The Vikings fought with broad, double-edged swords about a yard long. The *hilt* was decorated with carving, and a ridge called the blood channel ran down the length of the blade. The Vikings gave their best swords fanciful names—Fire of the Sea Kings and Gleam of Battle, for example—and fathers proudly handed them down to their sons.

On their side, the Indians used what might be described as a buzz-

bomb. It was the blown-up bladder of a moose, which was hurled from the end of a long pole. The buzz-bomb made so much noise when it hit the ground that when the Vikings first encountered it, they fled in panic.

Some historians believe that Vinland was located in what is now Maine or Massachusetts. Others think it was in the present-day Canadian province of Newfoundland. Evidence of the Vikings' presence in North America comes mainly from the remains of a settlement found in 1961 near what is now St. Lunaire, Newfoundland.

According to several sagas written by Icelanders long after Viking times, a number of settlements were established in Vinland over a period of about 20 years. However, no maps or other records of these early immigrants have survived, and their deeds were mostly forgotten over the years.

By the 1400's, the principal Portuguese ship was a small vessel called

Viking warships—also known as long ships—sailed well in rough seas. This example—now in a museum in Norway—is about 75 feet (23 meters) long and is made mostly of oak.

the caravel. Seagoing caravels were 60 to 85 feet (54 to 76.5 meters) in length and were made of sturdy oak, with a deep keel. A typical three-master had square sails on the first two masts and a *lateen*, or triangular, sail on the rear mast. Such an arrangement made it possible for ships to tack into the wind, however clumsily. Caravels were steered with rudders in the ships' sterns.

Other important technology included the magnetic compass, a device for determining direction. In this compass, a magnetized needle—mounted on a pivot so it turns freely—points in the direction of the earth's magnetic north pole. Mariners also had the astrolabe. A forerunner of the sextant, an astrolabe was used for measuring the angles of celestial bodies above the horizon. Together, the compass and the astrolabe made it possible to chart the seas.

Portuguese Success. In the 1400's, Portugal became a leader in navigation among European nations, due in large part to Prince Henry the Navigator. Serious and studious as a youth, Henry had a special interest in mathematics and astronomy. During his lifetime, he sponsored more than 50 expeditions, although he went on none of these voyages himself.

One of Henry's goals was to expand Portugal's trade and influence along the African coast. Henry, as a faithful Catholic, also felt it his duty to spread his faith, as did all such rulers. In addition, the Portuguese monarchy hoped to break the trade monopolies held by the Italian and Arab merchants of the time. Henry hoped to find the source of gold that Islamic traders had been carrying north from central Africa for hundreds of years.

Prince Henry the Navigator—seen here in an illuminated manuscript—did many things besides encouraging various explorers. For example, Henry and his brothers Duarte and Pedro were knighted after they pleased their father by capturing the Moroccan city of Ceuta in battle.

In 1441, one of Henry's explorers returned to Portugal with some Africans he had captured on an expedition.

In planning his numerous expeditions, Henry gathered together mapmakers, astronomers, and mathematicians of many nationalities at Sagres, Portugal. Even after his death the navigational knowledge gained under Henry's direction led to several historic expeditions, including the voyages of the Portuguese explorers Vasco da Gama and Bartolomeu Dias.

Portuguese ships reached the Madeira Islands in 1419 and the Azores in 1431. By 1460, the year of Henry's death, the Portuguese had explored the west African coast as far south as present-day Sierra Leone. Less than thirty years later, in 1488, a ship commanded by Bartolomeu Dias rounded the Cape of Good Hope at the southern tip of Africa, passing from the Atlantic to the Indian Ocean. An ocean route to all the riches of India and China now lay open. Scarcely 10 years after that, in 1497, Vasco da Gama led four ships from Lisbon around the Cape and continued east, finally reaching the west coast of India on May 20, 1498.

Over the years, the voyages of Dias and da Gama proved exceedingly fruitful for the Portuguese. They established colonies or trade outposts on both the west and east coasts of Africa, as well as in India, Sri Lanka,

Settled by the Romans in the 200's B.C., Genoa was already an old city by the time Columbus was born there. Long an important city-state and a strong naval power, Genoa eventually became part of the newly formed Kingdom of Italy in 1861.

Columbus himself drew this map of the island of Hispaniola, the second largest island in the West Indies. Today the Republic of Haiti and the Dominican Republic are found there.

Malaysia, Java, and China, and on the Moluccas—the fabled Spice Islands themselves. For many years, the Portuguese enjoyed great profits from their monopoly on trade in these parts of the world.

Columbus as a Young Man.
Other explorers also dreamed about finding routes to the East. One of these was Christopher Columbus, who conceived of a shorter, easier route to China and India that involved sailing due west instead of east.

The eldest of five children, Christopher Columbus was born in Genoa, Italy, sometime between August 25 and October 31, 1451. His father was a wool weaver, but a seafaring life appealed to Columbus much more. When he was about 19 years old, Columbus went to sea for the first time. Over the next few years, he sailed throughout the Mediterranean and made several Atlantic voyages in Portuguese ships, one taking him as far away as Iceland.

Columbus in Portugal. Just
when Columbus developed his beliefs about the distance from Europe to Asia is unknown. He mistakenly believed the distance to be much shorter than it actually is, and he pressed his possible supporters based on this mistaken belief. He first sought support for such a voyage from the king of Portugal, John II, in the early 1480's.

The king's councilors advised John II against the scheme. Portugal already was committed to finding an ocean route via the south and east. Besides, the councilors believed that Columbus had seriously underestimated the distance from Portugal to China and India. Future endeavors proved they were right.

Columbus based his calculations partly on his correspondence with Paolo Toscanelli, a learned man of Florence. Columbus' calculations placed Japan and Portugal only 3,000 nautical miles apart, and he reckoned that it was a western journey of only 2,400 nautical miles from the Canary Islands, in the Atlantic Ocean south of Portugal, to Japan. Actually, the distance from the Canaries to Japan is about 11,000 miles. Given the scanty storage space on ships of the day, and the limited chances for replenishing supplies during the trip, no ship's crew would be able to endure such a long voyage, even if splendid weather prevailed all the way. John II turned Columbus down.

SOME EARLY EXPLORERS

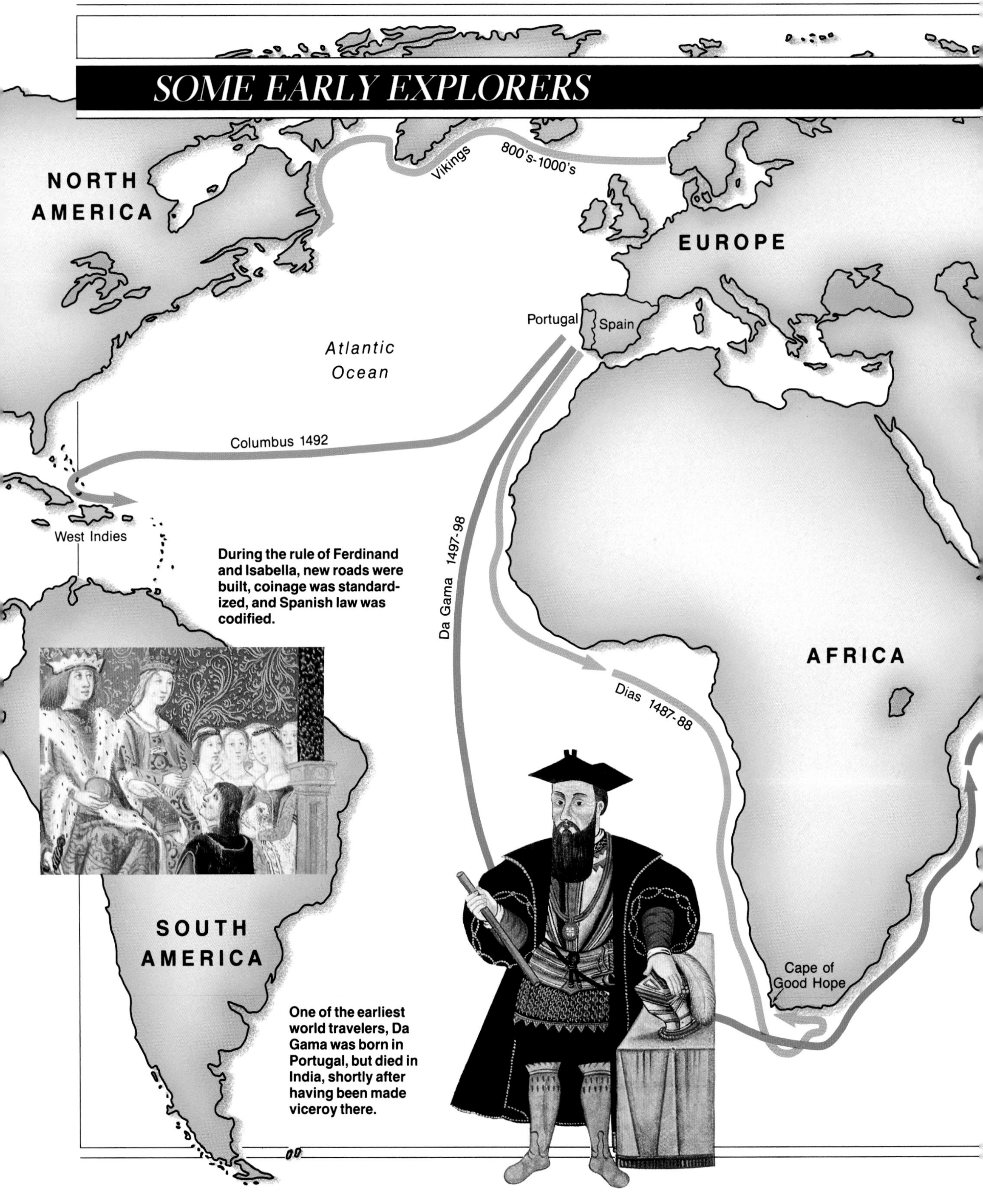

NORTH
AMERICA

EUROPE

Vikings   800's-1000's

Portugal   Spain

*Atlantic
Ocean*

Columbus 1492

West Indies

Da Gama 1497-98

During the rule of Ferdinand
and Isabella, new roads were
built, coinage was standard-
ized, and Spanish law was
codified.

AFRICA

Dias 1487-88

SOUTH
AMERICA

Cape of
Good Hope

One of the earliest
world travelers, Da
Gama was born in
Portugal, but died in
India, shortly after
having been made
viceroy there.

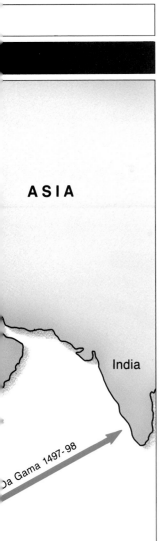

ASIA

India

Da Gama 1497-98

Indian
Ocean

Columbus in Spain. Columbus soon took his plan to the court of King Ferdinand and Queen Isabella, who had unified most of Spain under their rule and were now in the final phase of Spain's centuries-old conflict with the Moors. Only one Muslim stronghold remained—the Kingdom of Granada in the southern part of the peninsula.

Columbus reached Spain in the middle of 1485, and finally had an audience with Queen Isabella in the city of Córdoba about a year later, in May 1486. The queen seemed sympathetic. If Columbus succeeded, Spain would reap many benefits from trade with Asia. She turned the question of supporting Columbus' plan over to a commission. Several years passed before the commission reported.

In the meantime, Columbus returned to Portugal in 1488 hoping once again to convince King John II. Columbus arrived just in time to witness Bartolomeu Dias and his three caravels sail up the Tagus River as they returned triumphant from their journey around the Cape of Good Hope. Portugal now had its route to the Indies. John II had no further interest in Columbus.

At last Queen Isabella's advisers made their report late in 1490. Their conclusion was the same as that of King John II's advisers—no. Such a voyage as Columbus proposed was impossible because the actual distance was much greater than Columbus imagined.

In January 1492, Spanish armies conquered Granada. The long war against the Moors was over. Columbus, who had not given up entirely on Spain, had one more audience with the king and queen shortly thereafter. Again their answer was no.

Columbus, however, refused to quit. He maintained a steadfast faith that his calculations on distance were correct, that the voyage he proposed was feasible, and that he could suc-

ceed. He prepared to leave Spain to seek support from Charles VIII of France.

Before he got far though, a messenger from the queen caught up with him. Her treasurer, Luis de Santangel, had persuaded Isabella to change her mind.

In the end, Columbus chartered one ship himself with money he borrowed from relatives and friends. Queen Isabella obtained the rest of his fleet at no cost to herself. She simply announced that as a punishment for offending their imperial majesties, the port of Palos was to provide two ships, as well as crews. The queen did agree to foot the monthly payroll for the sailors, but again, it cost her nothing. She levied a special tax on the butchers of Seville and also used money confiscated from the Jews who had recently been expelled from Spain. All in all, Columbus' voyage—including ships, payroll, and supplies—probably cost less than $35,000.

The Historic Voyage. The *Santa María*, the *Niña*, and the *Pinta* set sail from Palos, Spain, on August 3, 1492, with some 89 officers and crew besides Columbus. As commander, he traveled in the *Santa María*, the largest of the three vessels. The ships reached the Canary Islands on August 12, where they took on more provisions and made some repairs. Then the tiny fleet left the Canaries on September 6 and did not sight land again for more than a month after they set out.

After three weeks of sailing westward, many in the crew wanted to turn back since this was by far the longest any Europeans had sailed in one direction without sighting land. On October 10, everyone agreed to sail on for three more days and then return if land were not found. Then, at 2 a.m. on October 12, land was sighted by moonlight. By noon that

day, Columbus had landed on an island in what is now the Bahamas and taken possession of a "New World" for Spain.

The three ships stayed only a few days at San Salvador, as Columbus named it. Then they sailed on. On Christmas Day, the *Santa María* was wrecked on a reef off the coast of present-day Haiti. The local Arawak chief helped save the cargo and seemed so friendly that Columbus decided to leave 40 men there to hunt for gold. On January 16, 1493, Columbus and the remaining two vessels headed home.

The voyage back to Spain was very rough, and the two ships became separated during a storm west of the Azores. The *Niña* so nearly sank that Columbus sealed an account of his discoveries in a cask and threw it into the water. Later, another storm tore off most of the *Niña*'s sails and forced it to land in Lisbon, Portugal, rather than Spain.

Columbus rode horseback across Spain to report his findings to Ferdinand and Isabella in the town of Barcelona. With him, he took some of his officers and a few Indians whom he had brought back from the "New World."

Ferdinand and Isabella gave Columbus a grand reception and confirmed his title of Admiral of the Ocean Sea, which gave him the authority to judge cases about such matters as piracy and shipwrecks anywhere in the Atlantic Ocean. He was also given the title Viceroy of the In-

dies, and he was ordered to make further voyages to colonize and explore the new lands.

By 1504, Columbus had made three more voyages to what became known as the West Indies. Yet it is doubtful that he ever realized that the land he had come upon was not the Indies, but the approaches to two continents previously almost unknown in Europe.

Columbus himself was a complex man who had a mystic belief that God intended him to make great discoveries. As a persistent man with a radical idea, he faced mutinous sailors, terrible storms, and later, inhospitable Indians, without flinching.

Yet, no one thought to name the "New World" after Columbus. That honor went to another Italian, Amerigo Vespucci.

The Legacy. Columbus' voyage to America ranks among history's most important events. It led to lasting contacts between Europe and America and opened new windows to science and knowledge.

Few people have had as great an effect on the world as Columbus. Yet no one thought to name the "New World" after him. That honor went to another Italian, Amerigo Vespucci. Although some historians doubt Vespucci's account, he claimed to have "sighted a vast continent" in 1497, concluding that it was part of a new continent. A German mapmaker named Martin Waldseemüller accepted the claim and in 1507 suggested that the "New World" be named *America*, after Amerigo. The name stuck.

Many scholars believe that the portrait of Columbus (shown opposite) is the most authentic one in existence today.

On March 9, 1500, Pedro Cabral and his fleet set sail from Portugal, heading for India. The ships probably looked much like the one shown here. The expedition got lost and finally landed in Brazil, which Cabral claimed for Portugal. There is some evidence that Cabral had never sailed a ship before.

CHAPTER 5: DISCOVERIES AND CONQUESTS

Hoping to prevent disputes between Spain and Portugal over land in the Americas and Asia, Pope Alexander VI drew an imaginary dividing line known as the Line of Demarcation in 1493. Spanish rights lay to the west of the line, Portuguese to the east. In the Americas, the Portuguese portion included only a small part of what is now eastern Brazil. The line, though, was adjusted the next year to give Portugal more land in what became its only colony in the Western Hemisphere.

In 1500, Pedro Álvares Cabral set out from Portugal in command of 13 ships bound for India. Veering farther west than planned to catch favorable winds, the fleet came within sight of what is now Brazil, and Cabral claimed it for Portugal. Along the coast, the sailors found a unique tree that had the color of a glowing ember—*brasa* in the Portuguese language. Later, brazilwood was widely used for making red and purple dyes.

Brazil bore several different names in its early years. The first was *Terra de Vera Cruz*, or Land of the True Cross, which was the name given by Cabral. King Manuel of Portugal changed the name to *Terra de Santa Cruz*, or Land of the Holy Cross. The name Brazil was officially adopted in the mid-1500's, despite opposition by the Catholic Church.

Early maps, however, identified the country as "Land of Parrots." The

On Sept. 25, 1513, Vasco Núñez de Balboa became the first European to see the eastern shore of the Pacific Ocean. Four days later, he waded into the ocean and claimed it and all the land around it for Spain.

59

area where Cabral's fleet put in contained huge groves of trees inhabited by dozens of varieties of macaws. The Portuguese were exceedingly impressed by the birds' large size and brilliant colors, to say nothing of their loud shrieks. They sent thousands of parrots back to Europe along with brazilwood, and they painted macaws on their maps of Brazil.

Brazil was also unofficially known as "The Land of the Southern Cross." The name came from the brilliant constellation of the Southern Cross that the astronomer on Cabral's ship described as pointing the way for future voyages to Brazil.

The Pacific Ocean and Florida. Another explorer, Vasco Núñez de Balboa, heard stories about a new ocean on the western side of the "New World." In 1513, he led an expedition across the Isthmus of Panama and, from a mountaintop, became the first European to view the eastern shore of the Pacific. He claimed all the land it touched for Spain.

In 1513, Juan Ponce de León sailed from Puerto Rico in search of the fabled Fountain of Youth. It was said that its waters would keep a person young forever. The quest led de Leon to "discover" what is now Florida. The Fountain of Youth, though, remained a dream.

Conquest of the Aztecs. In 1504, a Spaniard named Hernando Cortés arrived on the island of Hispaniola. Over the years, he and other Spaniards heard tales of a rich Indian empire in Mexico. Finally in 1519, Cortés launched an expedition to locate it. The Spaniards landed first on the Yucatan Peninsula. Then they sailed north along the coast.

Cortés and his army marched inland from the coast to the city of Tenochtitlan, where Aztec Emperor Montezuma II welcomed Cortés lavishly. At first, the Aztecs believed that Cortes was Quetzalcoatl, their most honored god, who had departed but had promised someday to return. Montezuma offered the Spaniards

In 1521, the Aztec empire was destroyed by Spanish conquest. This drawing by an unknown Aztec artist shows Aztec warriors trying to recapture a palace. The jaguar and eagle costumes worn by the warriors were badges of high honor and showed that they had taken many prisoners in earlier battles.

many objects made of gold, which they eagerly accepted.

However, there seemed no end to the Spaniards' desire for gold, or to their condemnation of the Aztec religion with its many gods and human sacrifices. The Aztecs soon realized that the Spaniards meant to conquer and loot their empire and destroy their religion. Less than a year later, the Aztecs rose up against the invaders and, following a bloody battle, drove them from Tenochtitlan. Cortés regrouped his army, and joined by more Spanish soldiers and by local enemies of the Aztecs, he attacked the city. It fell to the Spaniards in 1521 and was soon destroyed.

A Voyage Around the World.

Meanwhile, a Portuguese sea captain named Ferdinand Magellan had concluded that a route to the Indies around the southern tip of South America would be shorter than the trip around southern Africa. He persuaded King Charles I of Spain to finance the voyage, and Magellan sailed from Spain with 5 ships and 241 men in September 1519. Proceeding south along the coast of South America, the ships beat their way through a stormy strait and into the Pacific Ocean. Magellan named the sea *Pacific*, which means peaceful, because it seemed so calm after the passage through the strait.

The trip lasted until 1522—some three years—and brought great suffering to the crews. Magellan himself died in the Philippines in 1521 when he took sides in a struggle between warring Filipino groups. Finally, one lone ship—the *Victoria*—returned home. It arrived in Portugal on Sept. 6, 1522, with just its captain and 17 crewmen alive, but its cargo of spices more than paid for the trip.

The voyage had covered 50,610 miles (81,449 kilometers), so Magellan's route to the Spice Islands proved to be longer—not shorter—than the

one around the southern tip of Africa. Yet, the voyage resulted in greater knowledge of the earth and the Europeans' understanding of the Pacific Ocean. It also added the Philippines to Spain's dominion.

Other Spanish Conquerors.

Meanwhile, the Spanish explorers were learning from each other. As Balboa's chief lieutenant on his trek across Panama to the Pacific Ocean, Francisco Pizarro heard stories about treasures of gold far to the south. The area was, of course, the Inca empire.

This drawing of Tenochtitlan is thought to have been done by Cortés himself. Over the years, modern-day Mexico City arose on the site of the old Aztec capital. In 1978, though, excavation for a new subway system led to the discovery and preservation of the spectacular pyramid-topped temple called Templo Mayor that had stood at the heart of Tenochtitlan.

In both 1524 and 1526, Pizarro led unsuccessful expeditions to the south. Finally, in 1531, he and his men reached the Inca city of Tumbes on the Gulf of Guayaquil. At Tumbes, Pizarro learned that Atahualpa, the Sapa Inca, was encamped at Cajamarca, an inland mountain city about 200 miles (320 kilometers) to the southeast.

The Spaniards finally reached Cajamarca. In a surprise attack with their

base, he launched an expedition to search for gold in what is now the Southern United States. De Soto and a party of 600 soldiers traveled from Florida—through what are now the states of Georgia, South Carolina, Tennessee, Alabama, and Mississippi—to the Mississippi River.

Lusting for riches that did not exist, members of the De Soto expedition mistreated the Indians they met. They tortured many of the Indians

Pizarro promised to spare Atahualpa's life in return for a huge treasure of one room filled with gold and another filled twice over with silver.

horses and firearms—neither of which the Incas had ever seen—the Spaniards spread confusion in the Incan army. Thousands of Incan soldiers were killed, and Atahualpa was captured.

Pizarro promised to spare Atahualpa's life in return for a huge treasure of one room filled with gold and another filled twice with silver. The Incans paid the ransom, but to no avail. Fearing Atahualpa would rally his people against them if he were freed, the Spaniards executed him in 1533.

Accustomed to direction and close supervision from the top, the Incans were lost without the Sapa Inca. Within a short time, the Spaniards had conquered the Inca empire and gained fabulous wealth from it. Eventually, the Spaniards controlled much of the rest of South America too.

Another explorer, Hernando De Soto, had been a captain under Francisco Pizarro in the conquest of Peru and had become rich from the many treasures collected there. De Soto, though, wanted more.

In 1537, De Soto became governor of Cuba. Using the island as a

and held some of their leaders for ransom. For this, the invaders were rewarded with heavy losses in a battle with some Indians near present-day Mobile, Ala. De Soto himself died of a fever in 1542. Although he found no gold, De Soto was the first European to sight the Mississippi. Also, his expedition gave Spain a claim to much of North America.

While De Soto explored the Mississippi, Francisco Vásquez de Coronado led an expedition through what is now the American Southwest. In Mexico, Coronado had heard stories about great wealth in the Seven Cities of Cibola, said to lie somewhere to the north. Coronado set out in 1540 and traveled through parts of what are now Arizona, New Mexico, Texas, Oklahoma, and Kansas. He found many Indian villages, but no golden cities as he had hoped.

However, it was probably from these early explorers such as Coronado that the Indians first obtained horses. In the long run, horses made possible the widespread occupation of the Great Plains by nomadic Indian groups who lived by hunting buffalo.

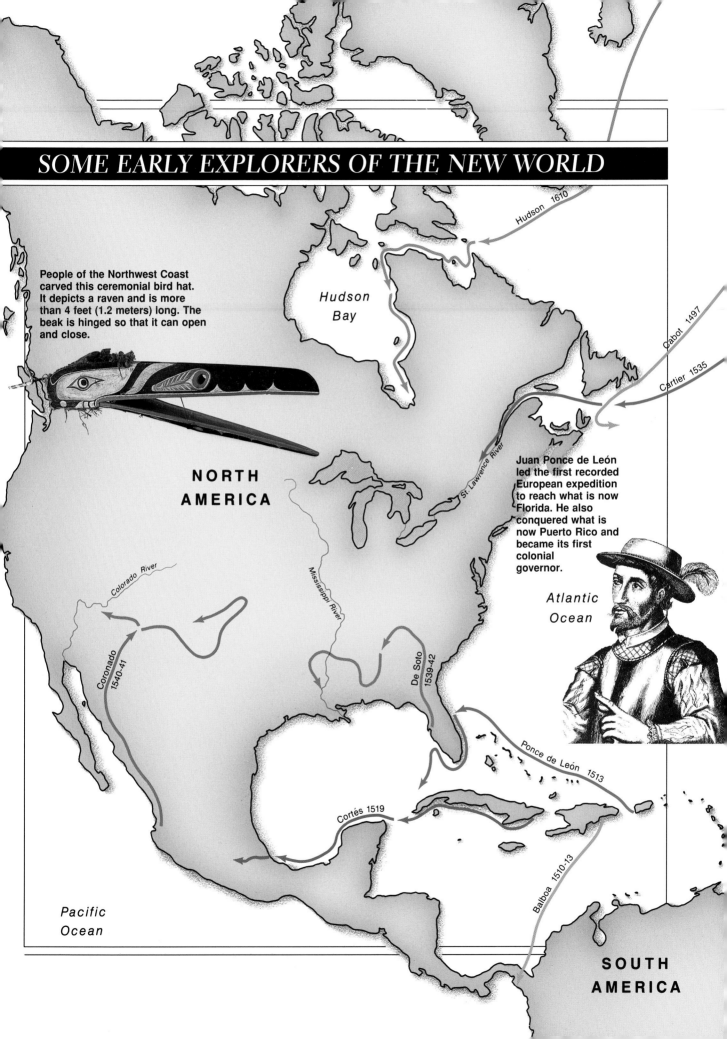

SOME EARLY EXPLORERS OF THE NEW WORLD

Hudson 1610

Cabot 1497

Cartier 1535

Hudson Bay

People of the Northwest Coast carved this ceremonial bird hat. It depicts a raven and is more than 4 feet (1.2 meters) long. The beak is hinged so that it can open and close.

NORTH AMERICA

St. Lawrence River

Juan Ponce de León led the first recorded European expedition to reach what is now Florida. He also conquered what is now Puerto Rico and became its first colonial governor.

Atlantic Ocean

Colorado River

Mississippi River

Coronado 1540-41

De Soto 1539-42

Ponce de León 1513

Cortés 1519

Balboa 1510-13

Pacific Ocean

SOUTH AMERICA

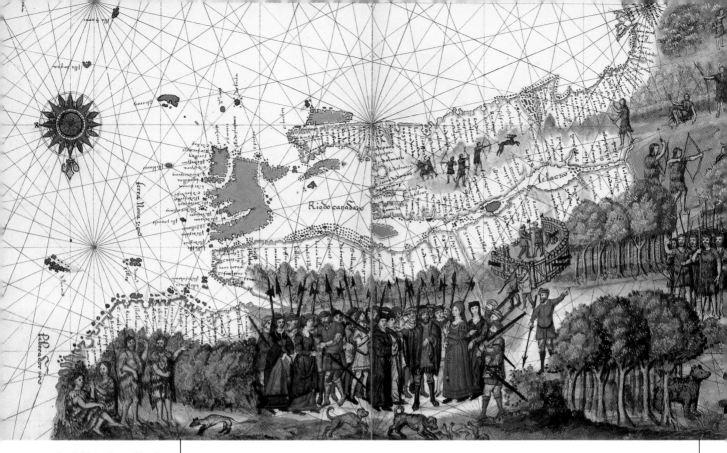

In 1546, the Vallard Atlas published this map showing Jacques Cartier landing in Canada. Cartier is in the middle wearing the red hat and short black coat.

Explorers for Other Nations. Five years after Columbus's first voyage, an Italian made a voyage of discovery on behalf of England. Known to us by the Anglicized name of John Cabot, he believed that Columbus had reached the Indies. He also believed, however, that a shorter route existed.

Sponsored by King Henry VII of England, Cabot set out across the Atlantic in May 1497. He reached land about a month later, dropping anchor either at what is now Newfoundland and Labrador or at Cape Breton Island—which Cabot thought was part of Asia. The only wealth he found was an abundance of fish in an area now called the Grand Banks. Although not considered very valuable at the time, the Grand Banks fish would attract many Europeans in later years.

The Northwest Passage. Magellan's ships had proved it was possible to reach the Indies from Europe by sailing around South America, but the journey was long and dangerous. Many Europeans came to believe that there had to be a better route. In France and England, attention focused on finding a shorter route—a Northwest Passage—through North America.

In 1534, King Francis I of France sent Jacques Cartier off across the Atlantic with two ships, telling him to look for gold and other items of value and a "Northwest Passage." Eventually, Cartier sailed into what is now the Gulf of St. Lawrence and landed on the Gaspe Peninsula, which he claimed for France. He also met some Iroquois Indians and took two sons of an Iroquois chief back with him to France.

In 1535, Cartier returned the boys during a second expedition. Then he and his men spent a severe and long winter on the St. Lawrence. Ice on the river held the ships fast in its grip, and several feet of snow covered the land. Unprepared for such weather, many of Cartier's men fell ill from scurvy (a disease caused by a lack of vitamin C), and some died. More would have died had not the Iroquois taught the French how to make a simple herbal drink, rich in vitamin C, that served as a remedy.

On this second journey—and a third in 1541—Cartier sailed up the St. Lawrence to a little beyond the present site of Montreal. When he found waterfalls there, he decided that the St. Lawrence could not be a passage across North America, and he returned home. Cartier found neither gold nor a Northwest Passage, but his voyages gave France a claim in North America and laid the foundation for a later colony.

Another explorer was Henry Hudson, an English sea captain. Between 1607 and 1611, he made four voyages to North America in search of a Northwest Passage—three for the English and one for the Dutch. During these trips, Hudson sailed along the coast of what is now North Carolina, into both Chesapeake and Delaware bays, and up the river that now bears his name in New York state.

Much farther north, Hudson came upon a body of water so huge he thought it must be the Pacific Ocean.

Instead it was a gigantic bay, and it, too, now bears his name—Hudson Bay. During the winter of 1610 in the Hudson Bay area, Hudson and his crew suffered greatly from hunger, cold, and disease. When spring came Hudson wanted to explore further, but his crew mutinied. The mutineers set Hudson, his son, John, and seven loyal crewmen adrift in a small boat. They were never seen again.

Ordinarily, sailors who mutinied against their captain were hanged if captured. In this instance, however, nothing happened to Hudson's crew when they returned to England. Although their guilt was obvious, they alone knew the supposed way to the Pacific Ocean that Hudson had discovered. In fact, not only were the mutineers not punished, but three of them became investors in a Northwest Company formed to explore Hudson Bay. Among the other investors was the archbishop of Canterbury.

By 1600, Spain had been in the colonizing business for a century. England, France, and Holland still lagged far behind, but explorers such as Hudson had helped them to catch up.

On Sept. 4, 1609, Henry Hudson sailed up what became the Hudson River. His ship called the Half Moon *fired its guns to scare off the curious, and possibly unfriendly, Indians.*

At the beginning of the 1400's, Portuguese sailors, eager to discover a sea route to Asia, faced the prospect of rounding the great western peninsula of Africa with apprehension. The

of long voyages such as those dreamed of by the Portuguese began to take shape.

During the A.D. 1000's, Mediterranean shipbuilders were perfecting the use of *lateens*, or triangular sails,

the sides of the stern.

By the mid-1400's, Mediterranean shipbuilders had developed a sailing ship that combined the best features of the cog and the lateen-rigged ship. The result was the *caravel*.

Caravels had three or four masts rigged with a combination of square and lateen sails. Like cogs, caravels had a sterncastle and forecastle and a rudder at the stern. This design became the basic style of vessel for overseas exploration. Columbus's *Niña* and *Pinta* were caravels, as were the ships commanded by such noted explorers as Ferdinand Magel-

lan, Francis Drake, and Vasco da Gama.

The development of navigational aids was as important to the advancement of ocean sailing as improvements in ship construction and rigging. The magnetic compass, probably first introduced into the Mediterranean region from China in the 1100's, was a great help in determining direction at sea.

To calculate their ship's position, early navigators used a combination of geometry and guesswork. They used an instrument called an *astrolabe* to measure the angle between a celestial body and the horizon. With this information, they

SAILING SHIPS

square-sailed ships in use at the time only sailed well with the wind. Along Africa's west coast, however, north winds prevailed: very effective for propelling a ship south along the coast, but an almost insurmountable obstacle on the return voyage.

Since about the time 3000 B.C., seafaring peoples, such as the Egyptians, Minoans, and Greeks, had worked to develop ships both sturdy enough to carry large cargoes over rough ocean waves, and maneuverable enough to sail under variable wind conditions. However, it was not until the Middle Ages that the possibility

This 1493 colored woodcut from an illustrated collection of Christopher Columbus's letters depicts Columbus discovering the West Indian Isles.

which were more effective than square sails for sailing into the wind. Meanwhile, shipbuilders in northern Europe were developing roomy, seaworthy vessels called *cogs*.

Cogs were sturdy ships with deep, wide hulls about 100 feet (30 meters) long. They had a single mast with a single square sail. At the front of the ship was a raised structure called a *forecastle* from which sailors could launch arrows or stones during warfare. A similar structure at the back called a *sterncastle* served as cabin space for important passengers. Cogs were steered by means of a single vertical rudder in the middle of the stern, a great improvement over the earlier steering mechanisms, which used oars fastened at

could compute their location on the globe.

Another method for estimating location was *dead reckoning*. Navigators considered the ship's speed, direction, and the length of time that had elapsed since their last known position to estimate the ship's current position. However, dead reckoning was not entirely reliable because changes in ocean currents, waves, and wind could greatly affect a ship's speed and direction.

As trade increased during the 1500's and 1600's, so did the size of ships. The principal Spanish vessel of the 1600's was a very big ship called the *galleon*. Its mainmast and foremast could hold up to three sails. Elsewhere, the major style of merchant ship became the *East Indiaman*, which was used for trade with Asia.

However, all ships still relied on sails and wind to get from one place to another. People had to wait until the 1800's for the invention of a faster and more dependable method of traveling the high seas—the steamship.

Sailors could fall victim to many fates, including fire. One man who traveled with Pedro Cabral in the 1500's kept a diary of the voyage. A page of the journal, shown above, contains the seaman's drawings of the burning and sinking of one of the expedition's vessels.

Sailors often used sextants, such as the pocket model at right, and compasses, such as the one above, to make their navigation decisions.

In 1539, work was begun on Morro Castle, at the tip of the island of Puerto Rico. Morro Castle was used as a temporary storage site for plundered gold that was being shipped back to Spain.

CHAPTER 6: SPANISH AND PORTUGUESE EXPLORERS AND COLONIES

"I and my companions," Hernando Cortés told the Aztecs, "suffer from a disease of the heart which can be cured only with gold." And Cortés did become wealthy from his share of plundered Aztec gold, as well as from land that was given to him by the king of Spain and the proceeds of a silver mine. He was, however, an extreme example of someone enticed by riches to explore. The opportunity for a better life lured most Spaniards to the colonies.

The Spaniards built many missions, such as the one in San Diego, Calif., shown on the opposite page. They also probably brought the first horses to the West, as evidenced by this drawing now preserved in Canyon de Chelley National Monument. They also took away a lot of gold, such as these tiny statues from Peru.

As one immigrant wrote home to his nephew, ". . . here men who know how to work and give themselves virtue make a living, and those who don't, don't."

Spain soon established two major administrative units, or viceroyalties, in the "New World." The Viceroyalty of Peru at first encompassed much of South America. It centered on Lima, a city that explorer Francisco Pizarro had founded in 1535 about 10 miles (16 kilometers) from the Pacific Ocean. Later, more viceroyalties were formed in this huge area. The Kingdom of New Granada stretched from what is now Colombia northward to present-day Panama.

The Viceroyalty of New Spain had modern-day Mexico as its center and included most of Central America and the West Indies. As the Spaniards expanded north, parts of what are now the states of Florida, Texas, New Mexico, Arizona, and California became part of New Spain.

The Immigrants: Who Came and Why. Only by colonizing the Americas could Spain hope to realize the full economic benefits of its new conquests. The government of Spain planned to import raw materials—especially precious metals—from the colonies and export finished goods back to the New World. In addition, Spain's Roman Catholic rulers felt duty-bound to convert the Indians to Catholicism.

Certain groups of people, regardless of wealth or skills, were largely kept out of the colonies because Catholicism was Spain's official religion. Spanish Jews and foreigners, especially Protestants, were not welcome either.

Letters from relatives in the colonies became a major factor in the continuing Spanish immigration. For example, a merchant in Mexico wrote:

> Now, nephew, I am advanced in years and can no longer take care of everything. I wish, if it please God, that you would come to this land . . . so that I could rest and you would remain in the business.

Female Immigrants. The percentage of female immigrants was never very large, at most 30 per cent in the late 1500's. In the 1600's the number fell, probably due to the natural increase in population among the colonists. Women settlers probably had expectations of a better life and hoped to improve their economic status. Young unmarried women and widows often hoped to find husbands who had achieved some degree of affluence in the "New World."

Making the trip across the Atlantic was not easy. One husband wrote to his wife that she should bring—for herself and for each child—a hundredweight of hardtack and the same of raisins, three cured hams, 25 pounds of fish, and half a peck of chickpeas, plus almonds, hazelnuts, sugar, two large jugs each of wine and vinegar, and one jug of olive oil. She was also told to bring "a good frying pan, a spit, a rolling pin and a ladle."

Social Classes. As in Spain, the colonial social system was hierarchical and based on birth. At the top of the social scale were the *peninsulares*—people born on the peninsula of Spain. The viceroy and top officials in the government, army, and church were all *peninsulares*. This upper class enjoyed privileges similar to those enjoyed by Spanish royalty, even when the individual *peninsulare* had neither competence nor wealth.

The Roman Catholic Church approved of marriages between Spaniards and Indian nobles. This picture is the announcement of such a wedding. The Inca bride and Spanish groom each wear their native dress.

There are not many drawings from the 1500's and 1600's that show the daily life of the Indians in South America at that time. Among the few that survived, this drawing shows them at work in the Potosí silver mine in Bolivia in the 1580's.

Next in importance were the *criollos*—Spaniards born in the Americas. Many *criollos* were wealthy landowners; others were merchants, doctors, and lawyers. Although denied the highest government offices, *criollos* were often minor civil servants.

The decided lack of female immigrants led to the creation of the next social class—*mestizos*. These were children who had one Spanish and one Indian parent. Although not near the top of the social order, the *mestizos* soon outnumbered higher social groups. By 1800, there were about 5 million *mestizos*, 3 million *criolles*, and 330,000 *peninsulares*.

The Indians.

The expanding Spanish colonies needed many workers. Thus strict control and use of the Indians seemed to be the answer. Under Spanish law, all non-Christians who were thought to be unlikely to accept Christianity were considered barbarians and could be enslaved. However, non-Christians who might become converts were viewed as pagans and thus as subjects of the Spanish Crown. Early on, Queen Isabella's religious advisers classified the Indians as pagans and potential converts to Christianity. Therefore, they were not to be enslaved. The queen declared the Indians to be her subjects "and free and not subject to servitude." However, the Indians were expected to pay tribute.

In the 1540's, the Spanish government set up a system called *repartimiento*. The system required every adult Indian male to work for a Spanish colonist for 45 days each year, usually in about one-week segments. Only a small percentage of the men from any one village were to be used at any one time, and the 45-day limit was intended to provide ample time for the Indians to work their own fields. Also, employers had to pay Indians for their work. However, the normal workday was often 12 hours long, the pay was not always forthcoming, and many colonists treated the Indians cruelly.

By the early 1600's, the number of Indians had greatly declined and *repartimiento* had ended. To attract

After the silver ore was dug out of the ground, it had to be melted down and refined. This drawing from about 1590 shows an Indian, a black slave, and a Spaniard all working together in a foundry.

workers, many Spanish employers offered to pay the Indians their wages in advance. However, the advance money offered was larger than the Indians would earn by doing the agreed-upon work, and the Indians were forbidden to leave their jobs until the debt had been repaid. With few other options, many Indians accepted the advance wages and thus became bound to their jobs for life. Even death was not a way out because a son was required by law to work off his father's debts. Soon a form of involuntary servitude had spread over the colonies as many Indians became *peóns*—a word that comes from the Spanish *peón*, meaning *day laborer*—in a system that remained common until the early 1900's.

A Terrible Toll.

Spanish rule took a dreadful toll in Indian lives. The exact number of people who died is not known, but the estimates are high. In general, the deaths were due to three factors: war, disease, and harsh treatment.

At first, almost all Indian groups fiercely resisted the Spaniards. However, most Indians were conquered by the Spaniards who had the advantage of guns and horses. A few groups remained free, however, including the Araucanians, who lived in what is now Chile.

The Araucanians, who originally fought the Spaniards with bows and arrows, clubs, spears, and pikes, learned to fight off Spanish cavalry charges by lengthening their pikes and attaching knives to the ends. Then the Araucanians got horses themselves, and soon their cavalry was an even match for the Spanish. The Araucanians also developed a horse-infantry in which two men were mounted on the same horse—the one in front held the horse's reins, while the one behind wielded a bow and arrow. Eventually, the Spaniards gave up trying to conquer the fierce Araucanians and accepted the Bio-Bio River, which flows into the Pacific at the

Ships filled with gold and silver regularly departed for Spain from ports on South America's eastern coast. Besides carrying precious metals, the ships also carried coffee, cotton, sugar cane, and tobacco. Over the years, Spain's economy became increasingly dependent upon the ships and their cargoes. Sometimes, the ship convoys were lost at sea or raided by pirates. Then the Spanish economy itself suffered some hardship.

modern-day city of Concepción, Chile, as the southern boundary of Spanish territory.

Hard labor in the silver mines and sugar cane fields also brought Indian deaths by the thousands. Even worse were the effects of diseases that had previously been unknown in the New World: smallpox, measles, and typhus. Tens of thousands of Indians died.

During the 1500's, the Indian populations of the Caribbean Islands were all but wiped out. For example, the Indian population of the island of Hispaniola fell from about 100,000 Indians in 1492 to only a few hundred by 1570. On the mainland, the area that is now central Mexico had an estimated population of 25 million when the Spanish explorers first arrived, but by 1580 it was reduced to just 1.9 million.

The decline in the Indian population was much the same in the Andes Mountains region of South America.

In the 1700's, the Indian population stabilized and even began to grow. By 1800, the Indians made up about 45 per cent of the total Spanish colonial population of as much as 14.5 million people. Nevertheless, the coming of the Spaniards literally killed millions of Indians, regardless of their age, sex, or attitude toward the conquerors.

The Portuguese in Brazil. Although the papal Line of Demarcation had given some of the "New

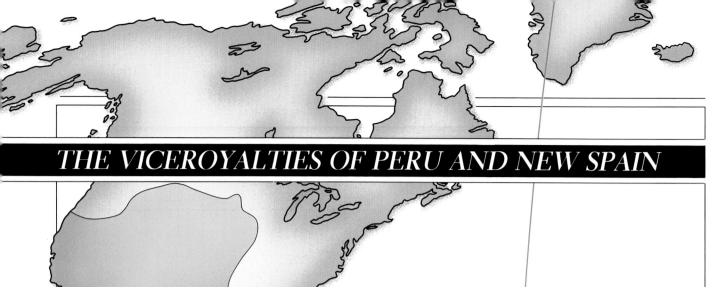

THE VICEROYALTIES OF PERU AND NEW SPAIN

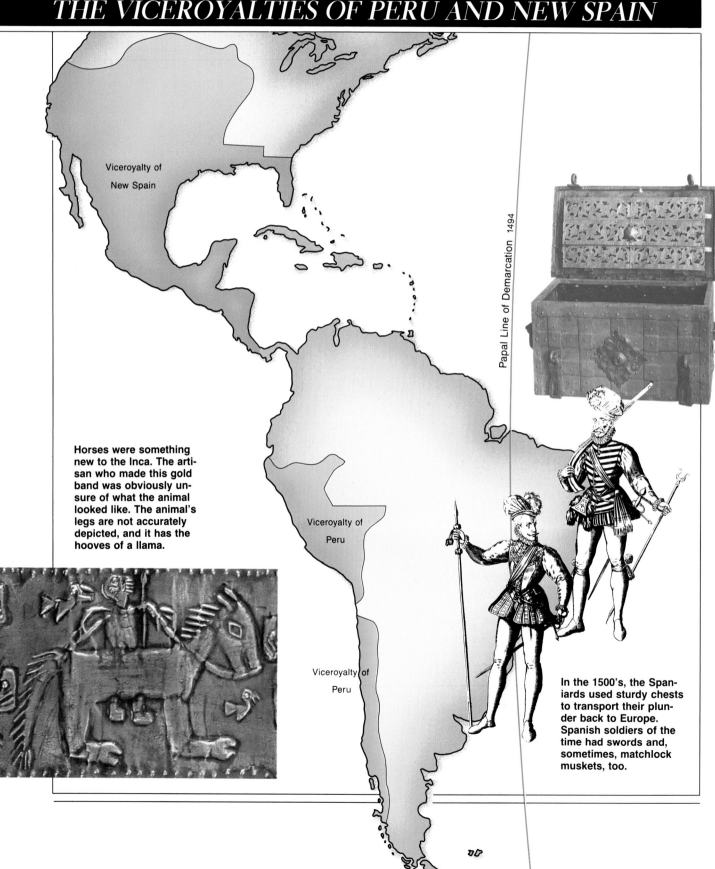

Viceroyalty of
New Spain

Papal Line of Demarcation 1494

Horses were something
new to the Inca. The artisan who made this gold
band was obviously un-
sure of what the animal
looked like. The animal's
legs are not accurately
depicted, and it has the
hooves of a llama.

Viceroyalty of
Peru

Viceroyalty of
Peru

In the 1500's, the Span-
iards used sturdy chests
to transport their plun-
der back to Europe.
Spanish soldiers of the
time had swords and,
sometimes, matchlock
muskets, too.

World" to Portugal, several decades passed before colonization began in earnest. By 1580, however, nearly 30,000 colonists lived in more than 15 settlements along the Atlantic coast, and there were about 120 sugar plantations in operation.

As the colonists spread into the interior, coffee, cotton, rice, and wheat also became important products. Until the end of the 1600's, though, sugar remained the principal export item.

In addition to the foods mentioned above, the Portuguese, along with the Spaniards, introduced a variety of animals to the "New World."

import African slaves to the "New World." For many years, Portuguese traders had been importing black Africans to Europe as slaves. The Portuguese, along with most other Europeans of the time, felt no compunction about making slaves of these peoples since they were regarded as barbarians and unlikely to adopt the Christian religion. Thus, the importation of African slaves to the "New World" was seen as merely an extension of existing practice, and the Portuguese remained the major supplier.

Historians have estimated that slave traders sent about 75,000 black Africans to the Spanish colonies in

---

As the Indian labor pool diminished, both the Spaniards and the Portuguese began to import African slaves to the "New World."

These included horses, dogs, cats, mice, sheep, donkeys, and mules. They also included the silkworm, together with the mulberry tree on which it fed. The Europeans introduced the garlic and the onion, as well as such aromatic herbs as mint, basil, marjoram, rosemary, and thyme. They brought many flowers, too, especially the rose.

The Indians' experience under the Portuguese was similar to their experience with the Spanish. European diseases caused many deaths, while the superior weapons of the Portuguese effectively conquered the Indians and put down uprisings. A general shortage of labor—combined with the reluctance of the Indians to work for the Portuguese—led the Portuguese to enslave the Indians.

Africans and Others. As the Indian labor pool diminished, both the Spanish and the Portuguese began to

the 1500's. By 1560, the Portuguese colony of Brazil had some 14,000 slaves. During the first half of the 1600's that number increased to around 125,000.

In the Spanish colonies the number of slaves grew even more rapidly. According to estimates, the number of African slaves rose to as many as 550,000 in the 1600's, while an additional 600,000 were imported during the 1700's.

Spain ruled Portugal from 1580 to 1640. During that time, immigration to the Portuguese colony of Brazil became much more diverse, though the newcomers still had to be Roman Catholics. During these years, for example, some 5,000 so-called New Christians immigrated to Brazil. These people were Jews who had converted to Christianity under duress. Many of these New Christians settled in the Brazilian province of Pernambuco and became merchants, plantation owners, and government administrators.

Early European explorers often built stone monuments when they claimed some new territory for their king or queen. This picture shows just such a monument in Florida in the 1500's. By the time the second group of explorers passed by, the Indians of the area had begun to worship the monument and leave offerings of food, weapons, perfumes, and medicines nearby.

The Spanish Frontier. Spanish influence in the "New World" was not limited to Central and South America. In 1565, Spanish explorer Pedro Menéndez de Avilés founded a small settlement and fort at what is now St. Augustine, Fla., the oldest continuous European settlement in the United States. St. Augustine served as a Spanish outpost and military headquarters in North America for two centuries.

In the 1680's, Frenchman René-Robert Cavelier, Sieur de la Salle, ventured into what is now east Texas, an area that the Spaniards believed was theirs. In 1690, the Spaniards founded a mission on the Trinity River near present-day Weches, Tex., to protect their claim to the area and in hopes of converting to Catholicism the Indians they found there. However the mission, called San Francisco de los Tejas, did not succeed, and the Spaniards abandoned it.

Mission activity continued, however, and by 1731, the Spaniards had established religious outposts in central, east, and southwest Texas. Some of these missions were accompanied by a *presidio* (fort). For example, on the site of the present-day city of San Antonio, the presidio of San Antonio de Bexar protected the mission of San Antonio de Valero. Some small communities of Spanish immigrants grew up around Texas missions, but by about 1800, Texas still had only 7,000 white residents.

Although Francisco Vásquez de Coronado had passed through present-day New Mexico and Arizona in the 1540's, Spanish occupation really began when a colonizing expedition led by Juan de Oñate headed north from Mexico in January 1598. The group included 8 priests, 129 soldiers, 83 wagons, 7,000 head of livestock, and an uncounted number of Indians. The colonists themselves consisted of about 400 men, accompanied by 130 wives and children.

When the Spaniards met the first Pueblo Indians, they demanded that they submit to Spanish rule, and the sight of Spanish weapons and horses helped convince the Indians to do so. The Spaniards then demanded food, since their food supplies were running very short.

The demand for food aroused the ire of a Pueblo group called the Acoma. The Acoma had built their pueblo on a huge rock some 350 feet (105 meters) high. In December 1598, the Acoma lured some soldiers seeking food into a trap, killed 13 of them, and then retreated to their practically impregnable pueblo.

The Spaniards attacked, destroyed the pueblo, and sold some 600 captured Acoma into slavery. For nearly a century after that, the Spaniards met with no serious resistance from the remaining Indians. Despite its military control of the area, however, the new colony failed to prosper. In addition, relatively few settlers moved to the new colony, and the local Indian population did not take well to their new masters.

The Indians resented the occupation and were hostile toward the Franciscan missionaries who tried to convert them to Christianity. Also, the Spaniards set up a system of forced labor and periodically sent groups of Indians south to work in the silver mines of New Spain, increasing the friction between the two groups.

In the late 1600's, the Pueblo Indians rose up in revolt and succeeded in driving the Spaniards from Pueblo territory. The Taos, Pecuries, Jemes, and other groups then returned to their traditional ways of life. Within a dozen or so years, though, the Spaniards had reconquered New Mexico. The region remained a Spanish frontier outpost into the 1800's.

California.

Beginning in 1697, the Spaniards established missions and other settlements in Baja California, the peninsula of present-day Mexico that lies south of the state of California. In 1769, Captain Gaspar de Portolá, the Spanish governor of Baja California, led an expedition that established the first presidio at San Diego. Portolá also founded a presidio at what is now the town of Monterey in 1770. Later, other settlers sent by Spain established more villages along the coast, including one at what is now San Francisco.

Spain did not have a strong hold on the region, however. Russia had fur-trading interests in Alaska and wanted to search for furs farther south along the Pacific coast. In 1812, the Russians established Fort Ross on the northern California coast—an action that led the fledgling United States government to create the Monroe Doctrine in 1823. In 1824, the Russians agreed to leave California, but did not actually do so until the 1840's.

The Missions.

The pope, as head of the Roman Catholic Church, granted the Spanish monarchs great authority over the church in the Americas. As a result, the missions became government agencies. The Spanish government paid the missionaries' expenses, hoping they

Acoma Pueblo, N.M., is believed to be one of the oldest continuously inhabited settlements in North America. It was probably founded in the 1300's.

could persuade the Indians to become loyal Spanish citizens, as well as Roman Catholics. Spain's two chief interests—the protection of its empire and the conversion of the Indians—usually determined when and where the missions would be founded.

Franciscan friars played a major role in the Spanish settlement of California. Franciscan Junípero Serra founded the first California mission, San Diego de Alcalá, near the present-day city of San Diego when Portolá started the presidio there. Serra went on to found 8 more California missions before his death in 1784. By 1823, some 21 missions had been built, each about a day's walk from the last.

Roman Catholic missionaries baptized millions of Indians in Mexico. Today, more than 90 per cent of Mexico's people are Roman Catholics, and religion plays an important role in the lives of most of Mexico's people.

Mission Life. The Spanish missions fed, clothed, and often housed the Indians who entered them. In return, the Indians agreed to take instruction in Christianity, observe Spanish customs, and work for the missions. The Indians were often forced to work very long hours, and they suffered from the diseases that they were exposed to. Many Indians became ill, and some died.

The missions included dining areas, schools, storerooms, and workshops as well as living quarters and a church. In most cases, these structures were made of adobe or stone and were arranged around a square courtyard. All the missions had farms, and many operated ranches. Some of the California missions developed into major agricultural and manufacturing centers. As one California traveler commented:

Over four hundred thousand horned cattle pastured upon the plains, as well as sixty thousand horses, and more than three hundred thousand sheep, goats, and swine. Seventy thousand bushels of wheat were raised annually, which, with corn,

Many of the old Spanish missions in America's West are major tourist attractions today. This lovely example is near Carmel, Calif.

beans, and the like, made up an annual crop of one hundred twenty thousand bushels.

In the mornings, mission Indians attended religious sevices and received instruction in the Catholic faith. During the rest of the day, they usually worked on the farms.

At first, many Indians welcomed the benefits of a more reliable and varied food supply, greater protection from their enemies, and the rich ceremonies of Roman Catholicism. Also, some Indians learned to read and write Spanish. However, many Indians disliked the highly structured mission routine and objected to being forbidden to leave the mission without permission. They also resented the missionaries' attacks on Indian religions and traditions, and they feared the diseases that killed so many of them. Some Indians fled. Others rebelled — often destroying the churches and killing the missionaries.

The System Changes. Many people in California and Mexico wanted the missions to be broken up. After Mexico became independent of Spain, the Mexican government seized and redistributed the mission properties in 1833 and 1834. The government began selling mission land to private citizens. By 1846, almost all the mission property had been sold, and their active role was ended.

PART 3: NEW FRANCE, NEW NETHERLAND, AND NEW SWEDEN

In the 1600's, three more nations appeared on the American colonizing scene. They were France, the Netherlands, and Sweden. France developed its major colony — New France — along the St. Lawrence River, where fur trading with the Indians became the main activity. Fur trading also lured early Dutch settlers to New Netherland and Swedish immigrants to New Sweden.

In May 1686, French explorer Sieur de la Salle happened upon a Caddo Indian village in what is now east Texas. This painting by George Catlin depicts the event.

Early fur trappers often lived near rivers for two reasons. First, that was where the highly prized beavers were. Second, the rivers were the major transportation route.

CHAPTER 7: NEW FRANCE

For many years after Jacques Cartier's voyages in the 1530's and 1540's, only fishermen came from France to what is now Canada. After hauling their catch aboard ship, the fishermen landed on the coast and laid out the fish to dry in the sun as a method of preservation. As a sideline, the fishermen began trading with the local Indians. The French wanted beaver pelts, which the Indians exchanged for knives, iron kettles, cloth, and other European goods. During the late 1500's, beaver hats became very popular in Europe, and an increasing number of Frenchmen crossed the Atlantic to trade with the Indians.

In 1604, a small group of Frenchmen began settlements in what are now mainly the provinces of New Brunswick, Nova Scotia, and Prince Edward Island in eastern Canada. Later in the 1600's, the small settlements developed into the fishing and farming colony of Acadia.

In 1608, Samuel de Champlain of France founded the settlement of Quebec on the St. Lawrence River.

The area immediately became a center for fur trading with the Huron, Algonquin, and other Indians. The French later founded an island trading post at Montreal. Upstream from Quebec, it lay near the rapids of the St. Lawrence River and at the mouth of the Ottawa River, which was the main waterway from the St. Lawrence into the interior. Soon, Montreal was the main trading post for beaver pelts.

By 1699, Quebec was a major city with churches, mansions, and monasteries. Almost a century had passed since the city had been founded as a fur-trading post by Samuel de Champlain.

On Oct. 10, 1615, Samuel de Champlain, his party of explorers, and some Indian allies attacked an Iroqois fort and village on Lake Onondaga in what is now New York state. The French built a movable shelter to protect themselves as they attacked the stronghold. The Indians set fire to the fort's walls. This drawing of the event was published in 1632 in Champlain's book about his exploits.

Conflict Over Fur Supply. In 1609, a Huron war party asked Champlain to join them in an attack on their enemies, the Iroquois. The Hurons had become important fur suppliers, so Champlain agreed and set off, taking two other Frenchmen with him.

The attackers met some 200 Iroquois of the Mohawk tribe in what is now upper New York state. The Frenchmen's guns were unfamiliar to the Iroquois and made all the difference. One blast of fire, smoke, and iron brought down three Mohawks, led to the capture of a dozen, and routed the remainder.

That brief encounter at what is now Lake Champlain turned the Iroquois into implacable enemies of the French, which they probably would have been anyway. The Iroquois and Hurons were ancient foes who both wanted to be the chief fur suppliers to Europeans. Now they became caught up in an economic power struggle between European nations that intensified the Indian tribes' enmity toward each other. The Hurons got to the

French first, and—more important—they controlled the vast region heavy with beaver north of the St. Lawrence River all the way west to Georgian Bay on Lake Huron.

As a result, the Iroquois turned to the Dutch, who were rivals of the French and had founded fur-trading posts in Iroquois territory early in the 1600's. The Dutch, and later the English, gave the Iroquois guns.

Nevertheless, the French fur trade flourished. In winter, the Hurons and other Indians trapped beavers and scraped and bundled the pelts. In the spring, the trappers set out for Montreal in huge *flotillas*, or fleets of small ships, along the Ottawa River and other streams. After trading and socializing for a few days, the Indians went home in their canoes, and another season of beaver hunting began.

Eventually, too much hunting reduced the beaver population, especially on the land controlled by the Iroquois. They then tried to monopolize the trade as middlemen to the Dutch and English. Other Indians, especially the Hurons, refused to cooperate and continued to supply only the French. Then the Iroquois hijacked Huron furs in transit and raided Huron villages as well as those of other Indians allied with the French. By the early 1640's, the Iroquois had almost wiped out the Huron, killing hundreds of them and destroying their villages and food supplies. The few Huron survivors fled west to the Great Lakes region. Many other Indians who were enemies of the Iroquois followed them.

During the later 1640's and much of the 1650's, the Iroquois menace slowed the French fur trade considerably. Settlers along the St. Lawrence lived in terror of Iroquois raids. Finally, the French government sent more than 1,000 soldiers to protect the settlements. Once they had mastered the Indian tactics of guerrilla warfare—ambush, sudden attack, hit and run—the French forces drove the Iroquois back.

The Great Lakes and Missionary Work. Beginning in the 1660's, the main supply of furs came from the Great Lakes region. Many of the Indians who had fled there had become successful beaver hunters again, while the lands near the St. Lawrence had been depleted of their supply of beavers. Soon the French came to rely on unlicensed traders known as *coureurs des bois* (vagabonds of the forest) and *voyageurs* (explorers). Many *coureurs des bois* became more or less permanent residents of the west. They lived with the Indians, learned their ways and skills, and married Indian women. Each spring, the *coureurs des bois*, like the Indians before them, sailed down the St. Lawrence in canoes loaded with beaver pelts. In late summer, they returned to their adopted homes. The

Early French settlers in the "New World" often lived harsh lives in primitive conditions. In addition to beaver, they sometimes hunted for fox. They also fished, especially for codfish, which they dried and then exported to Europe along with furs.

voyageurs had a slightly different role. These solitary men often worked for the fur-trading companies mostly by transporting the needed men and supplies to and from remote places.

By about 1600, fur-bearing animals were scarce in Europe, but the new middle class was hungry for luxury goods. The Europeans didn't so much want fur coats as they wanted felt hats made from the fur. Beaver pelts, with their thick and durable undercoats, were perfect for this purpose. Over the next several generations, hat styles repeatedly changed, but beaver remained the basic material from which the hats were made. In the late 1800's, silk hats became the fashion in Europe, causing the North American fur trade to collapse.

Religious Explorers and Colonizers. French missionaries also journeyed west. The first was René Ménard, who established a mission near what is now Keweenaw Bay on Lake Superior in 1660. Another missionary, Jacques Marquette, in partnership with fur trader Louis Jolliet, explored the Mississippi River. The two men wanted to learn whether the Mississippi flowed to the western ocean, and they reached the mouth of the Arkansas River before deciding it did not. Then Marquette and Jolliet turned back to the Great Lakes region. (In 1682, René-Robert Cavelier, Sieur de La Salle, led a party to the mouth of the Mississippi, where the French colony of Louisiana later developed.)

In its colonization, France—like Spain and Portugal—emphasized the introduction of Roman Catholicism to the Indians. Several religious orders, especially the Jesuits, participated in that work in New France. Although they often found their work difficult, many seemed to relish the experience. As one of the Jesuits wrote:

> The cold, heat, annoyance of the dogs, sleeping in the open air and upon the bare ground; the position I had to assume in their cabins, rolling myself up in a ball or crouching down . . . hunger, thirst, the poverty and filth of their smoked meats, sickness—all these things were merely play to me in comparison to the smoke and the malice of the Sorcerer.

The missionaries enjoyed their greatest success with tribes such as the Neutral, and especially, the Huron. They had next to no converts among the Iroquois. Instead numerous Jesuits were killed following prolonged torture at the hands of the Iroquois.

The Changing of Indian Life. In many ways, missionary activity in North America was much like that in Central and South America. In economic spheres, however, treatment of the Indians differed quite a bit. There were no large-scale farms, mines, or demands for huge numbers of laborers in New France. Consequently, there was no forced Indian labor or slavery. No conflicts arose when the French took over Indian land for their small farms and settlements, since the residents of New France used little land for these purposes.

The fur trade was the colony's economic base, and the settlers needed the Indians to maintain and expand that industry. However, the

When the rivers ended or went the wrong way, travelers had to pick up their canoes and carry them overland to the next good stream.

Imaginary scenes of fur-trading life often decorated the elaborate maps of the 1700's. This scene shows two settlers buying some fur pelts from an Indian. By the late 1600's, almost 100,000 beaver pelts were being traded per year. Traders sometimes made up to 2,000 per cent profit, unknown to the Indians.

settlers knew that the Indians would cooperate only if they were allowed to remain free and independent. There was no way to get the elusive Indians to trade furs except by giving them friendly treatment and a generous return in trade goods.

Still, just as slavery and other forms of forced labor changed the Indian ways of life in the Spanish and Portuguese colonies, so did the fur trade alter the Indians' cultures farther north. The Indians came to depend on the knives, awls, axes, kettles, cloth—and especially on the guns, powder, and ammunition—that they exchanged for their beaver pelts. The traditional Indian cultures and skills suffered as the peoples became less self-sufficient, and they lost some of their age-old atunement with nature. When they could, the traders also gave the Indians brandy, for the Euro-

peans soon learned it was much easier to strike a "good deal" with a drunken Indian than with a sober one. The missionaries condemned the practice and tried to prevent the introduction of liquor. Most of the time their protests had little effect. In addition, the Indians of New France also suffered heavily from smallpox and typhus, as did Indians elsewhere.

More Settlers and New Government.

The white population of New France increased slowly, growing from 359 in 1640 to just 675 a decade later. By 1663, as the Iroquois threat eased, the population reached about 2,500. Five years later, immigration had more than doubled the number of settlers, bringing the population of New France to 6,500.

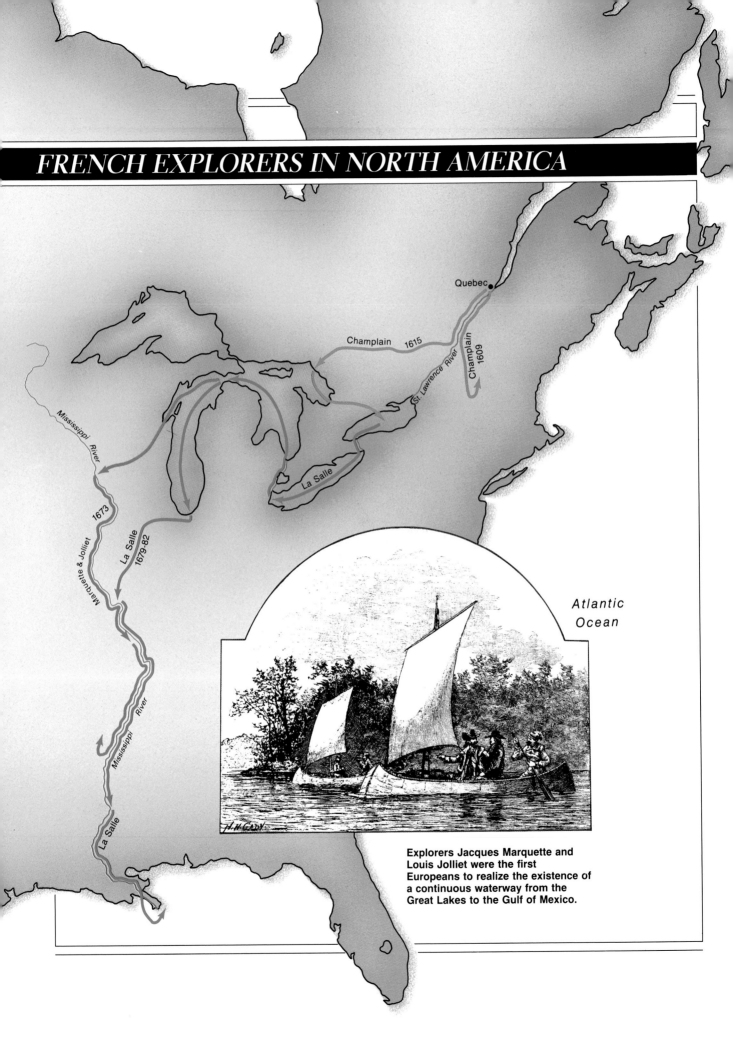

FRENCH EXPLORERS IN NORTH AMERICA

Quebec

Champlain 1615

St. Lawrence River

Champlain 1609

Mississippi River

1673

Marquette & Jolliet

La Salle 1679-82

La Salle

Mississippi River

La Salle

Atlantic
Ocean

H.N.CADY

**Explorers Jacques Marquette and
Louis Jolliet were the first
Europeans to realize the existence of
a continuous waterway from the
Great Lakes to the Gulf of Mexico.**

At the beginning, the government of the colony was in the hands of the Company of New France, officially led by a governor appointed by the king, but usually controlled by the company. In 1663, the French government abolished the company and made New France a royal colony, administered by a governor who was appointed by the king and a council. Its new royal status allowed the colony to attract more immigrants.

Under the new system, the government granted huge areas of land to nobles, religious orders, military officers, and merchants. The grants,

indentured servants who agreed to work for an established settler for three years and were then free to support themselves as they wished. The government also sent families of immigrants at its own expense.

Filles du Roi. From the beginning, New France was as short of immigrant women as other colonies were. However, the French government helped here, too, by creating a system known as *filles du roi* (daughters of the king).

> Word of the arrival of a shipload of *filles du roi* spread rapidly through the St. Lawrence settlements, and many bachelors met the ship at the dock to get a firsthand view of their prospects . . .

called *seigneuries*, generally covered from 12 to 100 square miles (31.2 to 260 square kilometers), usually running in narrow strips inland from the St. Lawrence. Those who received the grants were called *seigneurs*. They could, in turn, allot land to *habitants*—farmers who paid rent. The rent was usually a share of the crops, a fee, and several days' work for the community without pay. The French government also subsidized the passage of *habitants* and other immigrants to the colony.

The chance to have land to work at little initial expense attracted some French immigrants. As *habitants* they raised horses, cattle, sheep, goats, pigs, and oxen, all of which had originally been brought from France. They grew wheat, rye, corn, pumpkin, and tobacco, many of which the Indians had taught them to grow.

High wages lured skilled workers and artisans of all kinds to the colony. Some immigrants came as *engagés*—

In this system, government agents canvassed orphanages in France, seeking teen-aged girls who might be willing to emigrate. In exchange, the agents offered passage, clothing money, land, a cash dowry, and the prospect of finding a husband. For a number of years, ships arrived annually with hundreds of girls who had accepted the offer, and probably about 1,000 young women came altogether. Word of the arrival of a shipload of *filles du roi* spread rapidly through the St. Lawrence settlements, and many bachelors met the ship at the dock to get a firsthand view of their prospects for shedding single status. By 1669, the population of New France stood at around 4,000, and by 1700 it was about 15,000. However, immigration to New France dropped off after 1700. Thereafter, the colony depended mainly on natural increase among the settlers. In 1760, its population was about 65,000.

The settlers learned about snowshoes from the Indians. This engraving from 1722 shows a French voyageur out for a winter's walk with his musket, his snowshoes, and his pipe of tobacco.

Several factors caused this relatively small immigration to New France. First, France's immigration policy restricted the colony to French Catholics. Second, the area along the St. Lawrence and farther north was heavily wooded with oak and maple trees, and it took months of backbreaking labor to clear enough land for farming. Third, England had colonized the region to the south and, along with its Iroquois allies, blocked French efforts to expand in that direction. Fourth, no westward-flowing rivers gave easy access to the Great Lakes region. The fertile soil might have lured some immigrants, but only the Indians and fur traders seemed willing to endure the difficult journey to get there. Fifth, by emphasizing the fur trade, the French failed to develop a diversified economy. The fur trade actually involved relatively few people and offered only rough, wilderness life for most of the few who participated in it. Whatever wealth the beaver pelts did produce went mostly to investors and the French government, not to those involved in the actual work. Sixth, the *seigneurial* system, although it stimulated immigration to some extent, did not appeal to those who might wish to become—at least eventually—free and independent landowners. Finally, there was the climate.

Summers were short and often very hot. Heavy snowfall and bitter cold characterized the long winter season, during which the St. Lawrence River usually remained frozen for five months or more. All this seemed especially formidable to people who were accustomed to a milder, more temperate climate at home. In 1631, a Jesuit who had grown to like winter in New France described the scene around Quebec:

It has been fine because the cold has been severe. . . . The cold is sometimes so intense that we can hear the trees cracking in the woods, and it is like . . . gunfire.

The French settlers built their houses to cope with the weather. Instead of using stone as they had in France, they used wood, partly because it was more abundant but also because wood does not conduct cold. The settlers used stone only for the platform on which the house stood. The platform jutted out around the house so that dirt could be piled on top to insulate the building's base. Walls consisted of two layers of planks with a stuffing of hay between them for insulation. Roofs sloped sharply so as to shed snow.

The French Regime Passes. Between 1689 and 1763, France fought four wars—called wars for empire—with Britain. The conflicts included battles in Europe, in India, at sea, and in the American Colonies, where Indians fought on both sides.

The Acadians of Nova Scotia steadfastly refused to swear a loyalty oath to the British Crown, fearing that it would obligate them to take up arms against other French immigrants in

America in the event of another war. The British did not press the issue for a long time. However, during the last of the four wars—from 1754 to 1763—the British commander in Nova Scotia demanded the oath. Once again, the Acadians refused to pledge allegiance to Great Britain. This time their refusal spelled disaster.

The British commandant ordered the Acadians in Nova Scotia to leave. Armed with bayonets, British soldiers drove about 10,000 Acadians from their homes, forced them to abandon most of their possessions, and herded them aboard ships. Many families were broken up as the Acadians were scattered about in the British colonies to the south or sent back to France. Some 4,000 Acadians immigrated to the French-held territory of Louisiana, where they maintained their culture in small communities in the bay-ous. (Descendants of these immigrants became known as Cajuns.) However, many of the Acadians eventually returned to their old homes in New Brunswick and tried to mend their shattered lives.

The British captured Quebec in 1759, and the French and Indian War ended in 1763 with France's defeat. The vast lands France had claimed north of the St. Lawrence then became British Canada. However, this huge area, reaching from ocean to ocean and as far north as Hudson Bay, was only one claim that was soon relinquished. In 1803, France sold the vast Louisiana Purchase to the United States. The Louisiana Purchase was the largest land acquisition that new nation would ever make. With the sale, the nation of France gained some much-needed revenue, but its only colonies in North America were lost forever.

On Sept. 13, 1759, British troops defeated French forces at Quebec by attacking the city from the side along the St. Lawrence River. Both opposing generals, the Marquis de Montcalm of France and James Wolfe of Britain, were fatally wounded in the battle. At the request of the townspeople, French General Jean-Baptiste Ramezay surrendered the city to General George Townshend on Sept. 18.

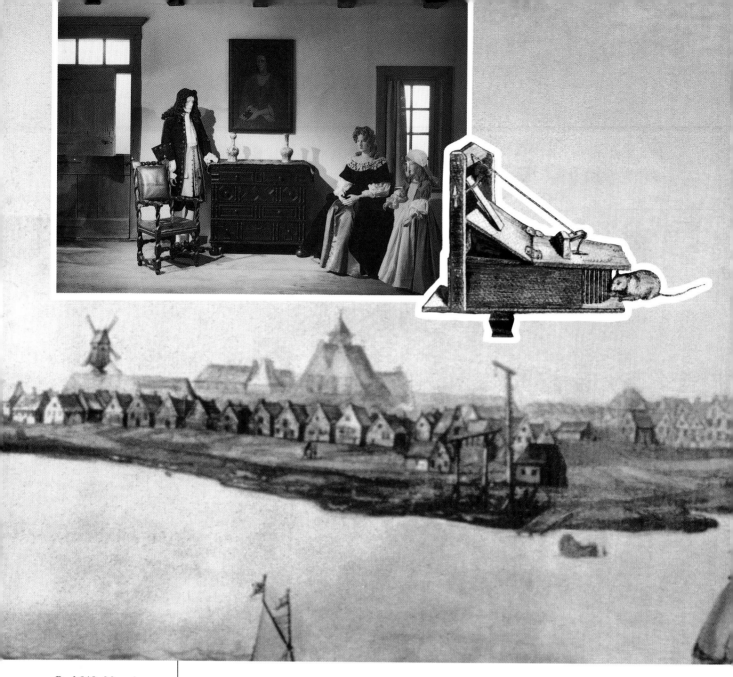

CHAPTER 8: NEW NETHERLAND AND NEW SWEDEN

The Netherlands was only a small nation bordering the North Sea in northern Europe, but even so, as a trading nation it was a serious rival to much larger European powers when it came to trading. Chartered in 1602, the Dutch East India Company sent ships on diverse voyages such as across the stormy Baltic Sea and around the southern tip of Africa and on across the Indian Ocean to engage in the East Indies trade. Interested in finding a shorter route to the Indies, the Dutch East India Company merchants hired Henry Hudson to search for one. Instead, he gave the Dutch a foothold in the Americas.

The wealthier residents of New Amsterdam, as shown at left, had homes with curtained windows. Both rich and poor alike, however, owned a mousetrap.

Peter Stuyvesant lost his right leg to a cannonball during a battle on the Caribbean island of St. Martin. He often decorated his wooden leg wth silver nails and lace.

The Dutch claimed a region in what is now the Northeastern United States and named it New Netherland. They soon followed up their claim by sending traders up the Hudson River, where they built Fort Nassau and began trading for furs with the Iroquois. The Dutch fur business was well timed—one year earlier, France's Samuel de Champlain had aided a Huron war party that fought the Iroquois. This alienated the Iroquois, so they were pleased to turn to the Dutch for trade goods.

In 1621, the government chartered the Dutch West India Company to oversee trade and colonization in America, and some 30 families arrived in 1624. A few settled on Governor's Island, others along the east bank of the Delaware River. Floods had demolished Fort Nassau, so 13 families were sent up the Hudson River to begin a new fort, Fort Orange, on the site of present-day Albany, N.Y.

More Dutch ships soon arrived, one bringing 105 head of livestock, another carrying 42 more immigrants. Within a year, New Netherland had a population of about 200 people. In 1626, immigrants began the settlement of New Amsterdam on the southern tip of Manhattan. The Dutch had purchased the island from Indians who may have been Mahican for a small amount of trade goods such as kettles, awls, and axes.

New Amsterdam.

By the later 1640's, the colony of New Amsterdam had a population of about 1,000. The residents included a few farmers among them, but most people were merchants, government officials, or

Peter Stuyvesant.

In 1647, Peter Stuyvesant arrived in New Netherland to take over the governorship from Willem Kieft. By that time, Stuyvesant already had several years of military and civil service and had served as governor of the Dutch colony of Curaçao in South America.

As governor, Stuyvesant ruled autocratically, and he tended to act rather than to discuss issues. For example, selling liquor to Indians in New Netherland was forbidden, but the number of drunken Indians on Manhattan Island and elsewhere suggested that the law was more frequently broken than honored.

Unlike other immigrant groups, the Dutch looked on Sunday as a day of pleasure as well as prayer.

---

artisans. It was neither a particularly healthful nor particularly secure community. Pig styes and open privies filled the air with disagreeable odors, and the fort that was supposed to protect the town was often in a state of disrepair.

Unlike other immigrant groups, the Dutch looked on Sunday as a day of pleasure as well as prayer. Taverns, which always did a steady business, remained open on Sundays. It was customary for men to spend Sunday afternoons in local taverns drinking and talking with their neighbors.

Colonial immigration was slow because most Dutch people were fairly comfortable at home. People in the Netherlands enjoyed religious freedom. Economic times were good, and jobs were not difficult to find. Thus, the hardships of a two-month ocean voyage to an unsecure life in the wilderness held little appeal for many of the Dutch.

Stuyvesant ordered that drunken Indians be rounded up and kept in jail until they revealed the source of their liquor. He then acted swiftly to punish those who had supplied the liquor. Also, although the Netherlands government directed Stuyvesant to hold elections for certain posts in the New Amsterdam government, he ignored the directive and appointed the officials himself. "We derive our authority," he once said, "from God and the Company, not from a few ignorant subjects." In 1648, for example, he selected four wardens to inspect the city's chimneys for fire hazards. In 1658, he appointed some other men to patrol at night to watch for fires.

Peter Stuyvesant had his troubles with the Indians, too. A quarrel between an Indian and a colonist in a peach orchard led to the so-called Peach War, which cost the lives of 60 Indians and nearly as many settlers as well.

New Sweden. It also fell to Stuyvesant to deal with the Swedes who had settled on territory claimed by the Dutch. The Swedish government wanted a piece of North America, and it established the New Sweden Company so that Sweden too could benefit from the fur trade. The company hired Peter Minuit, a former governor of New Netherland, to lead an expedition of Swedish immigrants to the "New World." In 1638, the first 50 or so Swedish immigrants arrived in Delaware Bay.

The region in which the Swedes settled resembled their homeland, as it was covered with forests. As a result, two of the items the Swedes brought with them—the ax and the concept of a log cabin—enabled them to live more comfortably than most other immigrants.

The Dutch in New Netherland soon decided that the Swedish landing was an intrusion on Dutch territory. Governor Willem Kieft told Peter Minuit:

the whole South River of New Netherland has been many years in our posession. . . . Therefore, in case you proceed with the erection of fortifications and cultivation of the soil and trade in peltries or in wise attempt to do us injury, we do hereby protest against all damages, expenses and losses, together with all mishaps, bloodsheds and disturbances, which may arise in future time therefrom . . . we shall maintain our jurisdiction in such manner as we shall deem most expedient.

Having given warning, Kieft then elected to do nothing and maintained

Swedish and Finnish immigrants built the first log cabins in North America in 1638. Such homes were not only relatively quick and easy to build, they were also fairly comfortable to live in. Later, other groups of immigrants also built log cabins as they moved westward, at least until they reached the treeless Great Plains.

Governor Johan Prinz, called "Big Tub," used this large, elaborate silver drinking mug while he lived in New Sweden.

that stance for the remainder of his governorship—probably because he had little choice. At that time, Sweden and the Netherlands were allies in Europe in the Thirty Years' War. Armed action by New Netherland in the "New World" would have disturbed that European alliance.

In the meantime, the Swedes built Fort Christina on the site of the present-day city of Wilmington, Del. Some immigrants became farmers while others traded with the Indians who came to Fort Christina with pelts. By the spring of 1639, two ships had left New Sweden carrying some 2,200 furs. Unfortunately, this small cargo did not even pay for the shipping. The sale of the pelts in Holland brought about 16,000 Dutch florins, while the cost of shipment alone amounted to 46,000 florins.

Johan Prinz. New Sweden found its counterpart to Peter Stuyvesant in Johan Prinz, who became governor in 1643. Prinz was a large man whom Indians called "Big Tub" since he allegedly weighed 400 pounds. Like Stuyvesant, Prinz was an ex-soldier and more likely to act than debate. Prinz kept the colony's executive, legislative, and judicial affairs in his own hands, often acting sternly, but not arbitrarily.

Prinz built a fort to protect New Sweden, and he did what he could to shore up the listless colony. He encouraged the fur trade and tobacco farming, and he tried to build up the colony's livestock herds. However, his efforts bore little fruit, and the New Sweden Company lost money on the venture. When the Swedish government refused to lend financial assistance, Prinz gave up and returned to Sweden 10 years after he had arrived in America.

New Sweden never became a successful colony. The Swedes were as reluctant to move to New Sweden as the Dutch were to emigrate to New Netherland. The population of New Sweden never reached 200—and half of those people came from Finland.

The Dutch vs. the Swedish.
Competition from the Swedes cut into Dutch fur profits, and after the Thirty Years' War ended in 1648, the Swedish-Dutch alliance no longer mattered. Governor Peter Stuyvesant then decided to put an end to the competition.

Stuyvesant did not act hastily. Not until 1655 did he equip a fleet and set sail for Fort Christina. Describing the encounter, Johan Rising, New Sweden's last governor, wrote about the Dutch that:

> inasmuch as we had not sufficient strength for our defence . . . and were in want of both powder and other munitions . . . we concluded a capitulation with Stuyvesant . . . stipulating that . . . the Dutch should freely transport to Sweden both us, and as many Swedes as chose to accompany us, for we held it better that the people should be restored to their Fatherland's service than to leave them there in misery, without the necessaries of life.

However, the success of Stuyvesant and his Dutch fleet was short-lived. Less than a decade later, Peter Stuyvesant found himself in Rising's shoes, gazing out at the menacing guns of hostile ships.

In 1653, the Dutch built a wall across lower Manhattan to keep out the Indians. By 1699, the English had dismantled the wall and built Wall Street in its place. In 1792, the first stock exchange opened there. This drawing from about 1860 shows the thriving port that also developed in lower Manhattan.

Few small countries have held as prominent—and prosperous—a place in the world as the Netherlands did during the 1600's. That century was, indeed, the Golden Age of the Dutch.

THE PROSPEROUS DUTCH

In the 1300's and 1400's, the Netherlands was ruled by the French Dukes of Burgundy, but it became Spanish territory in the early 1500's. In 1581, the Dutch declared their independence from Spain, but they did not win recognition of their freedom until 1648.

By then, the Netherlands had become a prosperous country through trade, and it had developed a colonial empire. Between 1600 and 1650, the Dutch merchant fleet tripled in size, and about half the world's mercantile shipping fleet was made up of Dutch ships.

The 15th century Dutch painting *The Legend of Saint Eligius and Godeberta* includes jewelry and fine fabrics that indicate the comfort of life in the Netherlands. The branch of coral on the shelf in the painting signifies the wide travels of ships of the time.

Dutch traders sought new sources of goods in the East Indies during the 1500's. In 1602, Dutch firms trading in that region formed the Dutch East India Company, with headquarters at Batavia—now Jakarta, the capital of Indonesia. After company sailors and soldiers drove the British and French out of the area, the

company organized the Dutch East Indies as a colony. The company also took over Ceylon—now Sri Lanka—and colonized the southern tip of Africa. The company's ships ventured to Japan, and when the Japanese closed their doors to other European traders in the 1600's, they allowed the Dutch to remain.

In the Western Hemisphere, Dutch merchants formed the Dutch West India Company in 1621. In 1624, the

Dutch founded the colony of New Netherland, which consisted of parts of present-day New York, New Jersey, Connecticut, and Delaware. In 1634, they captured what are now the Netherlands Antilles and Aruba in the Caribbean from Spain. From England they took a colony in South America, which they named Dutch Guiana.

Trade brought wealth to the Netherlands. The standard of living rose and produced a middle class that enjoyed all the luxuries of the time. During the 1600's, painting was in a period of brilliance, and Dutch painters enjoyed the support of this new middle class, who could afford to buy works of art. The buyers favored paintings whose subjects reminded them of their own comfortable lives, and the style of Dutch painting at that time reflected these tastes.

Jan Vermeer was known particularly for his many small paintings of the interiors of taverns and homes. Vermeer often showed people engaged in household tasks. Franz Hals made his name as a portrait artist and did many paintings of groups of people.

Rembrandt van Rijn, the greatest of the Dutch masters, was born in Leiden in 1606 and did much of his work in Amsterdam. He was in particular demand as a portrait painter and produced a huge number of paintings, etchings, and drawings.

The Netherlands' success in trade and colonization caused much bitterness among the nations that competed with it. In the 1600's, England and France fought wars with the Dutch for trade and land. England ended Dutch activity in North America in 1664 when it took over New Netherland. England made peace with the Dutch in 1674, and by 1678 the Dutch had driven the French from their land. England and the Netherlands then joined to defeat France in two wars, the second ending in 1714.

More than 50 years of warfare had exhausted the Netherlands, and it had lost its control of the seas to the British. Over the next 250 years, wars with Great Britain and colonial independence movements gradually eroded Dutch colonial holdings, and the era of this prosper- ous, far-flung empire ended.

Today, only two reminders of the Golden Age of the Netherlands remain—the Caribbean islands of Aruba and the Netherlands Antilles. Both these tiny areas are self-governing members of the Kingdom of the Netherlands.

By the 1600's, Amsterdam was a busy, crowded seaport, as shown at left, where middle-class people, such as those in the painting above, lived. The painting, *The Arnolfini Wedding*, was painted by Jan van Eyck and shows the interior of a Dutch home, with its mirrors, chandeliers, and well-dressed owners.

PART 4: THE ENGLISH COLONIES

Misfortune dogged England's first attempts to found a colony in the "New World," and the future of even the first successful settlement was often in grave doubt. During a century and a half, though, English settlers created 13 colonies along the Atlantic seaboard. Some colonies were founded for religious reasons and others for material gain, but all attracted immigrants who hoped for a better life.

On May 6, 1607, English settlers arrived in three tiny ships near what is now Chesapeake Bay. These replicas of the ships are anchored in a Virginia park that was created in 1957 to honor the 350th anniversary of the arrival.

NOVA BRITANNIA.
OFFERING MOST
Excellent fruites by Planting in
VIRGINIA.

Exciting all such as be well affected
to further the same.

LONDON
Printed for SAMVEL MACHAM, and are to be sold at
his Shop in Pauls Church-yard, at the
Signe of the Bul-head.
1609.

This advertisement for Jamestown sought to entice the English to farm in the first English settlement. A fire in January 1608 destroyed most of the tiny village. A reconstruction shows what the settlement may have looked like.

CHAPTER 9: THE FIRST VENTURES

Richard Hakluyt, an English clergyman who lived from 1552 to 1616, never saw the New World. In fact, he never traveled farther than France, just 20 miles (32 kilometers) away across the English Channel. Yet Hakluyt knew more about the world, particularly the New World, than perhaps any other person of his time.

N icotiana
inferta in-
fundibulo
ex quo hau-
riunt fumũ
Indi & nau
cleri.

Hakluyt was a self-taught geographer and historian. He studied the reports of sea captains, sailors, explorers, and immigrants who had returned to Europe, and he personally interviewed many English sailors. Armed with the information he had gathered and with his own ideas about the "New World," Hakluyt himself became a teacher.

Hakluyt saw the value of new estates for the nobles and new markets and exotic products for English merchants. In 1589, he published his masterwork, *The Principal Navigations, Voyages, Traffiques, and Discoveries of the English Nation.* His book provided a wealth of information about lands far from England, including important facts about the geogra-

Sir Walter Raleigh was a soldier, explorer, poet, businessman, and, for many years, a favorite of Queen Elizabeth I. The colonists he sponsored soon learned about tobacco, which had been unknown in Europe.

phy, the flora and fauna, and the people who lived there. The section devoted to the "New World" became a take-off point for explorers planning expeditions. For more than a century, Hakluyt's book served immigrants as a guidebook. It helped them make preparations for sailing and told them something about what their destinations held in store.

Early Efforts to Colonize.

A close associate of Hakluyt's, Sir Humphrey Gilbert, was the first Englishman to try to start a colony in the "New World." After raising money from friends to help finance his expedition, Gilbert sailed from England in June 1583, in command of a fleet of

Raleigh's Colony.

Although disappointed by Elizabeth's response, Raleigh persisted. His first effort failed. In 1587, he tried again.

After arriving on Roanoke, John White, the colony's leader, soon returned to England for supplies. He left behind his granddaughter, Virginia Dare, who had been born 27 days after the colonists' arrival—making her the first English child born in North America.

When White returned to America in 1591, he found no colonists. The only traces of them were the letters CRO carved on one tree and the Indian name CROATOAN on another. Europeans never saw members of the settlement—now called the Lost Colony—again.

In December 1606, three small ships called the *Discovery, Susan Constant,* and *Godspeed* set sail from England with about 100 immigrants aboard.

---

five ships. Landing on Newfoundland, he claimed that region for England, thus reinforcing John Cabot's claim of 1497. At the onset of winter, however, members of the expedition became discouraged, sailed for England, and were lost in a storm at sea on Sept. 9, 1583.

In 1585, Sir Walter Raleigh, Gilbert's half brother and also a friend of Hakluyt's, financed the first of several expeditions to search for another site for a colony. The vast land area the expedition traversed was named *Virginia,* after Elizabeth I, the Virgin Queen of England.

In 1585, Hakluyt sent a petition to Queen Elizabeth I eloquently arguing for royal sponsorship of colonies. The queen agreed to colonization, but she kept the royal purse strings tightly drawn.

In 1606, a group of Englishmen formed a joint-stock company called the Virginia Company of London — usually known as the Virginia Company—to finance another attempt at colonization. King James I granted the company a *charter*—a license to operate—and land in America to sell or otherwise parcel out to immigrants.

In December 1606, three small ships called the *Discovery, Susan Constant,* and *Godspeed* set sail from England with about 100 immigrants aboard. The group included four boys and one Anglican minister but no women. Most of the men considered themselves to be "gentlemen" and thus looked down on manual labor. None of the immigrants were farmers, but they expected to do well in America. Most planned to then return to England to enjoy their profits.

For six weeks, winter gales storming in from the west lashed the ships, holding them within sight of England. Not until the weather cleared in February 1607 were they on their way again. On April 20, they finally sighted Virginia.

Then the colonists opened the sealed company orders that directed them to move up a river, to establish a settlement on high ground, and to build a strong fort.

Jamestown. The colonists built their settlement, Jamestown, in a swampy area from which mosquitoes carrying malaria might swarm in summer. They constructed a flimsy, three-cornered fort and chose to live in tents.

From the start, the immigrants were on bad terms with the Powhatan Indians of the area. Some time be-

C. Smith taketh the King of Pamavnkee prisoner 1608

In his Generall historie of Virginia, *Captain John Smith described his exploits in the "New World." This highly fanciful illustration from the book shows Smith supposedly single-handedly capturing the brother of an Indian chief while dozens of other Indians stand by and watch. Smith's book also included maps with imaginary land features that he had named for his friends, family, and patrons. Later mapmakers did not use Smith's work.*

The lovely Pocahontas, meaning "playful one," was the daughter of Chief Powhatan. In his book True Relation of Virginia, *John Smith wrote that she once saved his life when her father was about to kill him. In 1614, she married a settler named John Rolfe and later sailed to England with him to help raise funds for the struggling colonists. She was quite a sensation there, and she was presented at court. She later died of smallpox while waiting to sail back to America.*

fore, Spaniards had carried off a number of Powhatans to slavery in the West Indies, and to the Indians, the newcomers looked just like Spaniards. The Powhatans attacked the colonists as they landed, wounding two with arrows. The harassment continued off and on during much of the summer. However, the Powhatans brought the settlers corn during the first autumn.

The colonists fell into deeper trouble through their own foolishness, however. Instead of planting food crops to carry them through the winter, many colonists spent that first summer searching for gold and silver. Disease and skirmishes with the Indians thinned their ranks. George Percy summed it up:

Our men were destroyed with cruell diseases, as Swellings, Flixes, Burning Fevers, and by warres, and some departed suddenly, but for the most part they died of meere famine.

In June 1607, Captain Newport sailed back to England for supplies. When he returned to Jamestown early in January 1608, he found only 38 colonists alive.

Captain John Smith. John Smith became president of the governing council in September 1608, and soon he adopted dictatorial methods in an effort to fulfill his duties and turn the colony around. He decreed that those who did not work would not eat, thus forcing the settlers to build a secure fort and strong houses and to search for food supplies that the Powhatans had stored for the winter away from the Indian villages. Smith himself led groups of settlers to gather meat, corn, and fish from a friendly Powhatan chief known as Wahunsonacock. With Smith's prodding, the settlers just barely pulled through the winter of 1608-1609.

In October 1609, Smith was injured by a powder explosion and had to return to England. The 300 or so Jamestown colonists then faced the most dreadful winter of all—a period known as *the starving time.* There was almost no food. Quarrels with Wahunsonacock and his people brought death to 22 settlers. Starvation and disease killed many others. Supply ships arrived from England in May 1610. By then, all but 60 of the colonists had died. The fort was a ruin, and the colony was a shambles.

The Virginia Company decided to replace the council form of government with an appointed governor. Soon, Sir Thomas Dale was in charge of the colony. Dale, officially the deputy governor, led the colony from 1611 to 1616. At first, he ran the colony along military lines. Colonists marched out to work each morning and marched back home at night, and

Ætatis suæ 21. Aº.1616.

Matoaks als Rebecka daughter to the mighty Prince Powhatan Emperour of Attanoughkomouck als Virginia converted and baptized in the Christian faith, and Wife to the worꝏ Mʳ Tho: Rolff.

all shared equally in the food produced. However, this more or less communal system did not work very well, so Dale modified it. He continued to require that each individual make contributions to the group, but he also gave 3 acres (1.2 hectares) of land to anyone who wished to farm for himself. This arrangement led to an increase in production.

Tobacco: A Saving Crop. It could be said that tobacco saved the colony of Virginia. In 1612, a settler named John Rolfe planted some fine tobacco seeds he had acquired from the West Indies. The resulting Virginia tobacco found great favor in England, where men smoked it in pipes, as cigars, and as *cigarillos*—little cigars wrapped in paper—and chewed or sniffed it in a powdered form called *snuff*. Tobacco was soon Virginia's principal export.

King James I, however, hated the habit and roundly condemned it to all who would listen, saying:

> There cannot be a more base, and yet hurt-full corruption in a Countrey than is the vile use (or rather abuse) of taking tobacco in this Kingdome. . . .

However, addicted citizens ignored their sovereign and continued to puff. As they did, the Virginia colony prospered.

By 1620, colonists were producing wheat and corn in abundance, along with grapes and livestock such as hogs, cattle, and horses, but tobacco was the economic mainstay. Writing in 1619, John Pory, one of Jamestown's original settlers, had underscored the weed's value to the colony: "All our riches for the present doe consiste in Tobacco."

The cultivation of tobacco influenced life in Virginia in many ways besides saving the colony economically. For one thing, it made living in villages impractical. Farmers tended to move every five or six years as tobacco culture exhausted the fertility of their land. Only the owners of huge estates, or plantations, could afford to stay in one place, cultivating part of their acreage at a time. Yet tobacco was so important to Virginia's economy that it practically replaced money.

English Brides. As Virginia's wealth increased, so did its immigrant population. However, there were few

This woodcut from the 1600's depicts a tobacco shop in London. Most of the tobacco grown in the American Colonies was exported to England until the Revolutionary War began in 1775.

The Puritans believed that worship should emphasize Bible reading, personal prayer, and preaching based on the Bible, not on ritual. They also believed that churches should be organized and governed by elected councils, not by bishops as the Church of England was.

Englishwomen during the first decade or so. A few married women and a small number of personal servants composed the entire female population. In 1619, though, a ship from England carrying 90 marriageable young women docked at Jamestown. Male settlers who had worked company land were allowed to select a bride without having to pay her transportation expenses. Those who farmed their own land as well as that of the company had to pay the ship's captain in tobacco for the passage of their brides.

By the early 1620's, Virginia had about 4,000 colonists in Jamestown and nearby settlements. Then a devastating war with the Indians reduced that population drastically.

The Powhatan Strike. After the starving time, peace generally prevailed with the Powhatan under Wahunsonacock, but a few years after his death in 1618, his brother Opechancanough became chief. Concerned by the colonists' thirst for Powhatan land, Opechancanough resolved to drive them from Virginia forever, beginning with a carefully planned surprise attack.

The settlers intensified things when they murdered Nemattanew, a Powhatan war chief. On March 22, 1622, the Powhatan simultaneously attacked several points on the Virginia frontier. By the end of the day, 347 colonists were dead. The survivors retreated to Jamestown to prepare a surprise attack of their own. Instead of striking back immediately, though, the colonists allowed the Indians to plant corn that spring. Then, displaying unusual patience, they waited for the grain to ripen. At harvest time they attacked, destroying Indian cornfields and villages and killing many Powhatan.

Twelve years of sporadic warfare followed. The colonists and the Powhatan made peace in 1634, but

Opechancanough and his warriors renewed the fighting 10 years later, this time killing 300 colonists. Finally, the Virginians defeated the Powhatan and drove them beyond the western frontier.

Puritans and Separatists. Virginia had been founded as a profit-making venture. A joint-stock company financed the next English colony, too. In Virginia, though, religion, rather than material gain, rested uppermost in the minds of the settlers.

For centuries, Roman Catholicism had been the official religion in European countries. Governments supported it, and even kings were expected to obey the pope in spiritual matters. Dissenters were often persecuted for heresy. European religious unity began to disappear with the start of the Protestant Reformation.

England became a Protestant nation in the 1500's when King Henry VIII broke with the pope and created the Church of England. Within the Church of England, though, were some who wished to "purify" Anglican worship, and this group broke away and eliminated the elements they disliked from their own services. Eventually, these people came to be called *Puritans*.

Efforts to bring change to the Anglican Church made little headway. A radical Puritan faction saw no hope for reforming Anglicanism and wished to leave the church. These people were known as *Separatists*.

Conservative Puritans included landowners, doctors, lawyers, merchants, cloth manufacturers and workers, and some farmers. Separatists were mostly plain folk—small farmers and artisans. The English government persecuted members of both the Puritans and the Separatists for their unorthodox thinking, eventually driving many to conclude that the only way to achieve their religious goals was to emigrate from England to someplace else.

The Founding of Plymouth Colony.

In September 1620, the *Mayflower* sailed from Plymouth, England, with 102 passengers aboard. The Separatists were in the minority, numbering 41—17 men, 10 women, and 14 children. Most of the remainder seem to have been Anglicans. The Separatists called the Anglicans *Strangers* and themselves *Saints*.

The *Mayflower* was only 90 feet (27.4 meters) long and 25 feet (7.6 meters) wide at the beam. Passengers were crowded among baggage, barrels and tubs of salted and smoked beef, beer, pickled eggs, and other supplies. The 65-day voyage was also stormy.

The Mayflower II *re-creates how the original* Mayflower *is thought to have looked. The reproduction is anchored near Plymouth, Mass. Peregrine White, born on the* Mayflower *after it anchored in Cape Cod Bay, used the cradle that is shown. White's birth made him the first English child to be born in New England. As an adult, White became a captain of militia and settled in the village of Marshfield.*

In 1614, Squanto, a Patuxet Indian, was kidnapped by English fishermen and taken to Spain to be sold into slavery. He escaped, however, and made his way to England, where he learned to speak English. In 1619, he returned to his home and found that almost all of his tribe had been wiped out by disease. The few survivors had joined the Wampanoag tribe, which Squanto did also. He died of a fever himself in 1622.

Bad weather and navigation errors put the *Mayflower* off course, and when land was sighted on November 20, the crew and passengers discovered they were not off the coast of Virginia as planned. Instead, they were near an area John Smith had explored, mapped, and named New England several years before.

After skirting what is now called Cape Cod, the immigrants chose to land at a harbor on the west side of Cape Cod Bay that Smith had labeled *Plymouth* on his maps. Five immigrants had died and two babies had been born before the *Mayflower* reached the Plymouth site. Thus 99 Strangers and Saints landed on Nov. 21, 1620, to start Plymouth Colony.

The Mayflower Compact.

Before disembarking, the colonists created a framework for government. The plan—the *Mayflower Compact*—was signed by 43 of the immigrants. In it they agreed to:

> covenant, & combine ourselves togeather into a Civill body politick; . . . and by vertue hearof to enacte, constitute, and frame such just & equall Lawes . . . from time to time, as shall be thought most meete & convenient for ye generall good of ye colonie; unto which we promise all due submission and obedience. . . .

They then chose John Carver to be the colony's governor. The Mayflower Compact was the first immigrant document to provide for self-government in America.

As winter was already upon the settlers, the men immediately began felling trees and sawing planks to build strong shelters on shore. During this time, the women and children continued to live on the *Mayflower* as protection against the harsh climate. The men also built a storehouse.

The first winter in America was hard despite these early efforts. The colonists' supply of onions and cabbage, sources of vitamin C, gradually ran out. As a result, many settlers developed *scurvy* (a disease caused by the lack of vitamin C). The settlers also suffered from tuberculosis and pneumonia. The Plymouth record of death read much like that of Jamestown: "Of a hundred persons, scarce fifty remain, the living scarce able to bury the dead."

That spring, Plymouth residents were startled by the appearance of a lone Wampanoag Indian named Samoset who came in friendship. Samoset later returned with Squanto, who proved to be the last surviving Patuxet. Almost all the other Patuxet had died of disease accidentally brought by earlier Europeans. Under Squanto's instruction, the colonists learned to trap animals for food and to plant corn and other crops.

In many ways, corn was "a miraculous plant." Planting and harvesting it took up less than two months of a farmer's time, while an acre planted to corn yielded about seven times as much grain as an acre planted to wheat. In addition, corn was extremely resistant to disease.

Then, too, people were able to use every part of the plant. They stuffed their mattresses with the husks and fed the stalks to their cattle in winter. They made tool handles and jug stoppers from the cobs, which also served as the bowls of corncob pipes. Children scattered the kernels in the backyard as food for poultry.

The First Thanksgiving. A good harvest resulted in 1621, and a ship carrying 35 more immigrants, all Strangers, arrived from England in November of that year. In the autumn of 1621, William Bradford—the colony's governor—proclaimed a festival to celebrate the colony's success. Of course, we now refer to this event as the first Thanksgiving. Although Bradford personally had little but contempt for the Indians, they were invited to attend the festival. The Indians contributed to the feast and joined the Saints and Strangers in a menu of corn bread, duck, eel, goose, leeks, shellfish, venison, watercress, and wine.

At first, the Plymouth colonists held all land in common, just as the Jamestown settlers had under Sir Thomas Dale. However, this worked no better in New England than it had in Virginia. Not until each family received land for its own use in 1623 did the settlers' food production increase measurably. However, it was not until 1648 that the colonists paid off their debt to the merchants who had helped finance their voyage to America.

The first people of Plymouth Colony were long known as "Founders" or "Forefathers." Much later, they came to be called Pilgrims, a term that might have come originally from William Bradford, who wrote that when the immigrants left Holland "they knew they were pilgrims."

The first Thanksgiving was actually a festival that lasted three days.

Today, people who want to know what life was like in the 1600's can visit Plimoth Plantation in Plymouth, Mass. Plimoth Plantation is a living history museum that demonstrates the experi-

PLIMOTH PLANTATION

ences and concerns of the Pilgrims and the Wampanoag Indians on whose land the Pilgrims settled.

Plimoth Plantation contains three main parts: the *Mayflower II*, the *1627 Pilgrim Village*, and *Hobbamock's Homesite*. The *Mayflower II* is an accurate reproduction of the type of ship that transported the Pilgrims to the "New World." The Ship's Master is aboard to tell people about the trip. He speaks in the English dialect of the 1600's that is used throughout the village, too.

Nearby is *Hobbamock's Homesite*, the residence of the Wampanoag Indian man and his family that lived adjacent to Plimoth Plantation. Hobbamock taught the Pilgrims the best farming methods for the area and about the Native Americans nearby.

In the *1627 Pilgrim Village*, visitors can watch the modern-day "Pilgrims" go about their daily lives. The first houses the real Pilgrims built closely resembled the homes they had had in Europe. These first houses had thatched roofs, like English cottages. However, the Pilgrims quickly realized that wood was more plentiful than reeds or straw, and soon they were building houses with shingles rather than thatch. These sturdy houses usually had one chimney inside the framework that helped supply warmth in the cold New England winters.

Making clothing was an important task. It was usually the women who planted the flax, tended and harvested the crop, spun the yarn, and wove it into linen. The women also wove woolen cloth from the yarn spun from the fleece of sheep. The linens

Most Pilgrims ate bread and cold meat for breakfast and supper. The big meal of the day was served about noon.

Building homes and preparing food were important duties in the early colonies. Today, workers at Plimoth Plantation demonstrate these skills for tourists.

and woolens were colored with dyes made from berries, roots, walnut hulls, and certain barks.

Men usually wore breeches and a long linen shirt. Women usually wore a linen or wool dress, a petticoat, and single undergarment called a *shift*. Children wore much the same kinds of clothes as adults.

After the first few years, the colonists kept themselves better supplied with food than any other people in the world. They raised hogs, sheep, chickens, and cattle. They hunted deer and wild turkeys, and they collected clams, oysters, lobsters, and many kinds of fish from the nearby rivers and ocean. They also raised several crops, especially corn.

Corn was a basic food in almost every home, and corn bread was a special favorite. It was made by mixing corn meal with water or milk, salt, and lard and then baking it. Stew was another popular dish. It was usually made from meat and vegetables cooked together.

Today, the activities and traditions of the past are preserved at Plimoth Plantation, as well as at other living museums. These include Colonial Williamsburg in Virginia, Strawbery Banke in Portsmouth, N. H., and St. Marys City near Leonardtown, Md.

The homemade furnishings of a family were plain and strong. Sometimes, a shelf was used to display any dishes or pewter-ware a family might have.

Early colonial villages usually had just one main street that was lined with small sturdy homes.

In the 1600's, Anne Hutchinson left Boston for religious reasons and gained fame for her act. Another reformer, Roger Williams, once preached in this tiny church that was first built in 1634 in Salem, Mass.

CHAPTER 10: OTHER COLONIES FOR RELIGIOUS PURPOSES

As Plymouth Colony grew and its people prospered, it became an example of what settlers could accomplish in the "New World." Soon, many conservative Puritans in England concluded that emigration to America was the only road to religious freedom. At the same time, John Winthrop and others formed a joint-stock company to finance more colonization in hopes of reaping profits from the sale of "New World" goods.

To some extent, Puritan emigration was motivated by economic conditions as well as religious persecution. Depression had struck the market for English cloth, bringing hardship to the weavers, and the farmers had suffered several poor harvests in a row. Some weavers and farmers were Puritans, and other artisans and farmers were willing to join the Puritans in seeking a better life. However, religion was the major reason behind Puritan emigration, as the Reverend John White said in one of his writings in 1630:

> Necessitie may presse some; Noveltie draw on others; hopes of Gaine in time to come may prevaile on a third Sorte; but that the most, and most sincere and godly part, have the advancement of the Gospel for their main Scope I am confident.

John Winthrop, the colonial governor of Massachusetts, supported the banishment of both Hutchinson and Williams. However, such intolerance was found even as far south as Baltimore, shown here in 1752, which had started as a haven for Catholics.

The Puritans still hoped for Anglican Church reform. In the meantime, they planned to fulfill a mission by establishing a religious community that would serve as an example. As the Reverend Peter Bulkeley said, "The eyes of the world are upon us."

Establishing Massachusetts Bay Colony.

The Puritans had begun preparations for leaving England before Charles I, whom they opposed, dissolved Parliament. In 1628, John Endecott and a band of about 50 immigrants sailed to the "New World" and settled in Salem, north of Plymouth. Two years later, under Winthrop's leadership, about 1,000 Puritans sailed for America.

Like the Plymouth settlers, the Puritans suffered greatly during their first year in America. Eventually, they prospered, and by 1660, the colony held 40,000 souls.

The Puritans believed in going to church, praying, tithing, caring for the poor and sick, and providing children with a religious upbringing. They also believed in education and established Harvard and Yale colleges as well as many public grammar schools. In addition, they upheld what has been called the "Protestant ethic," making virtues of hard work and thrift.

Actually, the settlers of Massachusetts Bay had no choice about whether or not to work hard. Before immigrants could begin farming, they had to clear the land—and it took about a year to clear one to two acres. One reason was the stony quality of the soil, a leftover from the last ice age. Boulders were strewn everywhere, and most were heavy to shift.

Connecticut.

Soon after the settlement of Massachusetts Bay, the colonists began to itch for land that was more easily cleared and more productive—which led them to consider the Connecticut River Valley. Ships could travel for 50 miles (80 kilometers) up a river alive with fish, while the rich land on the riverbanks offered attractive sites for houses and farms.

The Puritan leaders of Massachusetts tried to discourage migration to the southwest. People who moved to Connecticut would be far from central government control and

strong Puritan religious influence. That did not deter residents of Newtowne, Watertown, and Doxbury who wished to establish new homes, however. They were more than willing to follow Thomas Hooker, Newtowne's pastor, and other leaders to the Connecticut Valley.

Hooker had arrived in Massachusetts in 1633 and had quickly become a popular and influential minister. He had more lenient views than John Winthrop and other Puritan leaders did about who should have the right to vote, hold office, and be admitted to church membership.

In the spring of 1636, a minister named John Warham and his congregation left Massachusetts to establish Windsor, Conn. Others left Watertown to make new homes in Wethersford. In May, Thomas Hooker and his Newtowne group set off for Hartford, where a few people from Massachusetts had already settled.

Connecticut attracted many immigrants, and the colony grew steadily. By the time of the American Revolution, the colonial population numbered 191,392. The number of Native Americans, though, was just slightly more than 1,000.

Rhode Island.
Soon after its founding, Rhode Island became known as "Rogues' Island" and as the colony where "people think otherwise" according to the "proper" people of Massachusetts Bay. "Otherwise-thinking" led to the colony's establishment and in part contributed to its appeal as a place to live. Rhode Island's beginnings, and its success, can be traced to its founder—Roger Williams.

Williams was 28 when he arrived in Massachusetts Bay in 1631. He soon established himself as a contrary thinker, insisting that the Puritans break completely with the Anglican Church instead of trying to reform it. He opposed Massachusetts laws that

Puritans shunned altars in their churches, so the pulpit was often the central focus instead.

forbade blasphemy as well as those that required church attendance. He believed the immigrants in Massachusetts had been wrong to simply take over Indian land without permission or any kind of compensation. Williams also believed in freedom of worship, and he did not think that the government should enforce any set of specific religious beliefs. All this went against Puritan thinking, and concerned Massachusetts leaders summoned him to appear before them to answer for his preachings.

Actually, a number of Puritan ministers privately agreed with Williams on one or more of the points he made, but none said so openly. Furthermore, the idea of independent congregations was sound Puritan doc-

The European settlers and the Indians had very different ideas about living and working. The Europeans cleared fields and used the trees to make fences for their individual plots, as shown by the painting near right. The 1585 watercolor drawing by John White, far right, includes no fences, and it shows how the Indians usually lived.

trine, though Puritan leaders did not follow it consistently. Nevertheless, the church leaders decided to rid the colony of Williams by sending him back to England. However, Williams learned of the decision. Before action could be taken, he and a few followers left Massachusetts in midwinter, heading south. After negotiating with the Narraganset Indians for some land, the group started the community of Providence.

No sooner had Williams left Massachusetts than controversy began to swirl around another freethinker—a woman named Anne Hutchinson—who had arrived from England with her family in 1634. In Massachusetts she continued to be a follower of Cotton Mather, a well-known Puritan minister.

In Boston, Hutchinson began to hold meetings after Mather's sermons to discuss and explain them, and this led to trouble with the Puritan authorities. More important, the authorities accused her of saying that nothing one could do, including obeying church and secular law, could merit the favor and love of God. God granted those as gifts to people whom He would save. According to her Puritan accusers, Hutchinson and her followers were *Antinomians* who stressed the mystical nature of God's free gift of grace. Soon, specific charges were brought, and a trial was held.

Actually, Anne Hutchinson had never argued against either church or civil law. At her trial, however, her explanations of numerous ideas seemed to suggest heresy. Most damning was the accusation that she believed a person could communicate directly with God, which was heresy to Puritans. The court ruled that she be banished from Massachusetts.

The story of Anne Hutchinson ended sadly. Her husband died in 1642, and she moved to New York. During a war there between some Native Americans and the Dutch, Hutchinson and several members of her family were killed.

Rhode Island was born in religious controversy, and the disputes continued. General agreement on religious liberty for all seemed to be the only thing that held together the rather diverse colony "where people think otherwise."

Controversy did not prevent Rhode Islanders from prospering, however. The people farmed, raised livestock, fished for seafood, built ships, and traded with England. By the 1770's, the tiny colony had about 60,000 inhabitants.

New Englanders and Native Americans.

The New Englanders concluded that Native Americans must be children of Satan, since they did not know about God. From the immigrants' point of view, the Indians' religious rites and ceremonies were simply "devil worship."

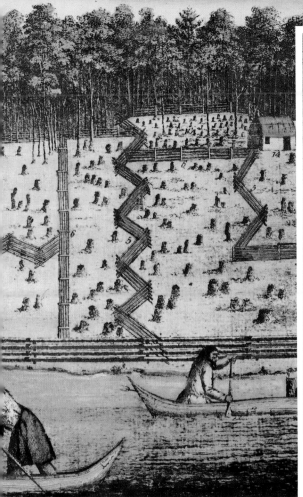

Missionaries in Massachusetts Bay and Plymouth Colony had some success with converting Native Americans, usually calling the converts "praying Indians." By 1675, about 1,100 converts lived in 14 separate towns known as "praying towns" which the missionaries had established for them.

In New England as elsewhere, Native Americans quickly came to rely on the cloth, ironware, shoes, and guns they received in trade for their beaver pelts and other items. These European trade goods helped to change the traditional Indian way of life in New England, just as they had in New France.

The Indians also traded land for colonial goods, and in the beginning at least, they had no objections to selling land. Their ideas about land ownership and ownership of most other possessions, however, differed quite a bit from those of the Europeans.

In Native American cultures, land belonged to the group, to be used by all. No one, not even the most powerful and respected chief, had the right to tribal land. The Indians believed that they sold the Europeans only the right to use the land for a time, and they expected to be able to continue using it themselves. To the Europeans, on the other hand, land ownership meant individual, exclusive rights of usage. They believed that a person who sold land no longer had any right to it.

The Native Americans could not comprehend the concept of private property. Nor could they fathom the idea of competition in pursuit of personal gain—something the Europeans valued highly. For their part, the Europeans did not understand the communal, cooperative Indian way of life. The cultural gap between the two groups was too wide to be bridged, and in New England, the conflict over land led to war with the Pequot in the 1630's.

The Pequot War. Conflict between the Pequot and the colonists erupted in 1636, when Massachusetts settlers accused the Pequot of murdering a colonist, although hunger for land and a sense of mission were probably the stronger, underlying causes. In any case, John Endecott led a raid on Pequot villages in retaliation. The Pequot responded by attacking the Saybrook settlement at the mouth of the Connecticut River and by carrying out additional raids near Wethersford.

The colonists, aided by Indians who were enemies of the Pequot, attacked a Pequot village near West Mystic, Conn., at sunrise on June 5, 1637. The attackers set fire to the village and burned between 600 and 700 Pequot alive. Others were killed as they fled the flames. In July, the colonists and their Indian allies trapped more Pequot in a swamp near Southport. Their Indian enemies tracked down the few Pequot who managed to escape, and the colonists sold them into slavery in Bermuda.

The most destructive conflict in New England, though, was King Philip's War, from 1675 to 1676. Philip, whose Indian name was Metacomet, had become chief of the Wampanoag in 1662, and he nursed a hostility toward the colonists for what he saw as their unfair treatment of the Indians. More important, Philip believed that the Native Americans would have no worthwhile future until the colonists had been driven from the land.

In June 1675, more than 4,000 Narraganset, who were formerly friendly to the settlers, joined Philip and his Wampanoag in an attack on Swansea, Mass. During the next year, both colonists and Indians raided villages, massacring hundreds on both

> ## The colonists, aided by Indians who were enemies of the Pequot, attacked a Pequot village near West Mystic, Conn., at sunrise on June 5, 1637.

sides, and the colonists captured Philip's wife and son and sold them into slavery.

New England forces finally trapped and defeated the Wampanoag and Narraganset in a swamp near South Kingston, R.I., ending the war except for scattered Indian raids that continued off and on until 1678. Philip escaped capture in the Great Swamp battle, but the colonists hunted him down and killed him in 1676. They dismembered his body, stuck his head on a pole, and carried it back to Plymouth where it remained on display for 25 years. Altogether, King Philip's War cost at least 1,000 New England lives and the destruction of 12 towns. Native American losses were equally heavy.

Penn's Holy Experiment. One other colony became as well known as Rhode Island for its religious freedom. This was Pennsylvania, founded by William Penn—primarily as a haven for members of the Society of Friends.

At age 22, Penn had joined the Society of Friends, a group also known as Quakers. Originally meant as an insult, the name *Quaker* came from a statement by George Fox, the Society's founder, who told an English judge that he should "tremble at the Word of the Lord." After that, the judge—and others—referred to Friends derisively as "Quakers."

Quakers believed that the *Inner Light* of Jesus dwells in the hearts of ordinary people and that each individual can communicate with God directly. Also, the Quakers had no formal ministry or designated churches; wherever they gathered became their meeting house.

As pacifists, Quakers refused to bear arms, nor would they tithe to the Anglican Church. These two examples of obstinacy were viewed as treason by the king, his advisers, and Anglican Church officials. As plain folk who believed in complete equality, the Quakers would neither doff their hats before their "betters" nor address them as "sir." Also, although Quakers believed women should be excluded from leadership positions, women did have complete spiritual equality. None of these attitudes sat well with the English and their class system.

William Penn made peace with the Indians in 1682, and in the early 1800's, Quaker artist Edward Hicks painted this romanticized version of the event. Necklaces, such as the one below, portrayed the peaceful meeting of the two groups and were given by the Quakers to the Indians to help keep the friendship strong.

The Quakers in England were persecuted as the authorities broke up their meetings and jailed them. At least 15,000 were thrown in English prisons, and many died there. William Penn spoke out for the Quakers and their beliefs both in speeches and in printed pamphlets. For his efforts, Penn was jailed on four separate occasions.

Instead of stamping out the Society of Friends and their so-called heresies, the persecution merely increased the Quaker ranks. Between 1660 and 1680, the number doubled—from 40,000 to 80,000.

Some Quakers left England for the colonies to escape persecution.

They settled into peaceful lives in Rhode Island and New Jersey, but in Massachusetts they were jailed and deported. The Quakers were not welcome in Virginia or New York either.

In 1681, as payment for a debt, King Charles II of England granted William Penn the land in America that became Pennsylvania. Penn made treaties of friendship with the Susquehannock and other Indians of the region, paying them for their land. Referring to Pennsylvania as "a holy experiment," he declared his colony open to any and all Christian persuasions. The colony prospered from the beginning through farming, industry, and commerce.

Quaker meetings were much the same in America as in Europe. This painting, called Gracechurch Street Meeting, *shows a Society of Friends gathering in London in the late 1700's.*

The major settlement in Pennsylvania was Philadelphia, and it quickly became a flourishing port. It was also a planned city, laid out by William Penn in a gridiron of streets, with regularly spaced squares filled with trees. Broad Street, like its name, was 100 feet (30 meters) wide. Other streets, which were 50 feet (15 meters) wide, were named after trees and fruits that grew in the area—Chestnut Street, Strawberry Street, and the like. Houses were built mainly of brick, but they were so narrow that a visitor wrote home saying that he much preferred a wooden house "that I may swing a cat around in."

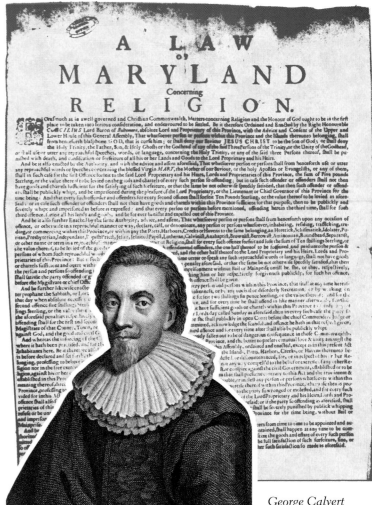

Maryland.

Maryland began when Charles I granted land and a charter to George Calvert, the first Lord Baltimore, in 1632. Calvert died soon thereafter, and the king then directed the charter to Calvert's son, Cecil, the second Lord Baltimore. The region was named after Henrietta Maria, Charles's queen.

In 1634, the first Maryland colonists sailed from England to found the settlement of St. Mary's City near the southern tip of what is called the Western Shore. With soil and growing conditions similar to those of Virginia, Maryland soon became a tobacco colony also.

Cecil Calvert was a Roman Catholic, and he planned to make Maryland a place of refuge for fellow Catholics—who were persecuted in England—as well as a home for people of all faiths. Calvert believed that any religious restrictions would hamper the colony's growth and development.

Religious toleration did not last long in Maryland, however. In 1654, Lord Baltimore lost control of the colony to a group of Protestant settlers led by William Claiborne, a fur trader. Calvert regained control four years later and promised to uphold the religious freedom guaranteed in 1649.

In 1689, the Calvert family again lost control of the colony in a Protestant rebellion when the Protestant Association seized control. The Association's leader demanded that England take control.

In 1691, the English Crown took over the colonial government and ruled through an appointed governor. The Calverts regained control in 1715 under the fourth Lord Baltimore, Benedict Leonard Calvert, a Protestant. Four years later, Maryland Catholics lost the right to vote and did not regain it until 1776. Until the Revolutionary War, Maryland remained in the hands of the Calverts.

George Calvert probably did not have any idea that his charter in 1632 would lead to documents such as Maryland's 1649 law concerning religion. It is often cited as a milestone of religious freedom. The law contains ideas that foreshadow the U.S. Constitution's Bill of Rights, which would come almost 150 years later.

James Oglethorpe first came to America in January 1733 with 114 colonists who included some persecuted Lutherans from Salzburg, Austria. This painting shows them leaving Europe for America with Oglethorpe in the lead.

During colonial times, every colony had an official seal that was put on documents to show their authenticity. The seal of the colony of Carolina, far right, was used until Carolina was divided into North Carolina and South Carolina.

CHAPTER 11: ROUNDING OUT THE 13

English fishermen who arrived in the early 1600's were probably the first Europeans in what is now New Hampshire. In 1614, Captain John Smith explored the islands off present-day Portsmouth. Although he named them Smith's Islands, they are now known as the Isles of Shoals. Smith's reports, plus the success of the Jamestown settlement by 1620, stimulated interest in beginning a colony north of Massachusetts.

David Thomson received the first land grant in the region in the early 1620's. In 1623, he led a band of immigrants that settled at Odiorne's Point, which is now a part of the community of Rye. At about the same time, a man named Edward Hilton founded the community of Hilton's Point, now called Dover.

In 1622, Sir Ferdinando Gorges and Captain John Mason received large tracts of land, which they sought to colonize. Gorges's land lay in what is now Maine. Mason's was in the region between the Merrimack and Piscataqua rivers, extending to the sea-coast. Mason named his land New Hampshire, after the county of Hampshire in England, the seat of his family's estate.

Like other landowners, Mason hoped to profit from his investment,

Weaving cloth became an important task in the colonies since fabric imported from Europe was very expensive. Today, visitors to colonial Williamsburg, Va., can watch people make cloth using the same methods the colonists used.

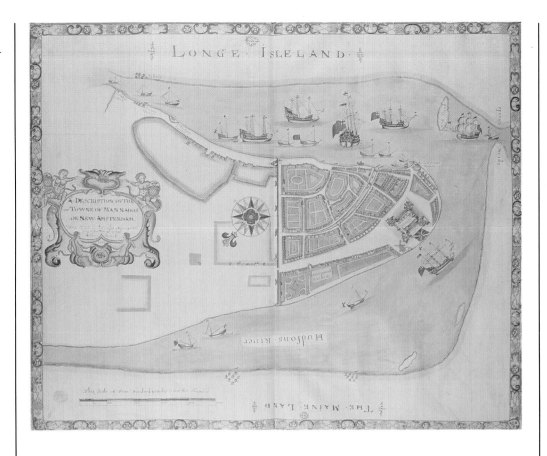

but shortly before his death, he complained that although he had expended a great deal of money, he had received not one penny in return.

A Colony Changes Hands.

Although stubborn, autocratic, and sometimes arbitrary, Peter Stuyvesant was an honest man and was considered by many to be the best governor New Netherland ever had. However, fate was unkind to him, for Stuyvesant was also the last governor of New Netherland, since he was forced to preside over the extinction of Dutch claims in America.

In March 1664, King Charles II of England gave his brother, James, Duke of York, all the land west of the Connecticut River to Delaware Bay, along with Long Island and parts of Maine and Massachusetts. As Lord High Admiral, the duke had all of England's warships at his disposal,

and he immediately organized a fleet of four men-o'-war to invade and conquer the territory. By the end of May, the ships had set sail under the command of Colonel Richard Nicolls and reached New Amsterdam in August.

Although most people of New Amsterdam took the news of impending invasion calmly, Peter Stuyvesant did not. The lace on his wooden leg danced and jiggled as he stomped around, fuming and blustering, trying to organize a successful defense — but to no avail. Nicolls demanded Dutch surrender, but offered to allow the people to remain in the colony and keep their land and other possessions. On September 2, John Winthrop, Jr., governor of Connecticut, came ashore with a letter for Stuyvesant:

> My serious advice therefore . . . is this, That you would speedily accept his Majesty's gracious [offer] . . . that you may avoid the effusion of blood . . .

Stuyvesant took Winthrop's advice and surrendered. James, the Duke of York, then changed the name of New Netherland to New York, and Richard Nicolls became its governor.

Still, for generations, the stamp of the Dutch immigrants remained. Haarlem remained Harlem, instead of Lancaster as Nicolls had wished to call it. Such words as *cookies*, *coleslaw*, and *waffles* remained embedded in common parlance, too.

New Jersey.

New Jersey, named after the Isle of Jersey in the English Channel, was a smaller plum that fell to the Duke of York. In June 1664,

The colony's population increased steadily. In just the 10 years from 1760 to 1770, it rose from about 94,000 to nearly 117,500 people.

Delaware.

In 1655, the land that encompassed Delaware passed from Swedish hands to Dutch. Less than 10 years later it went to English rule. It remained under New York jurisdiction until 1682, when the Duke of York granted the region to William Penn to become part of the Pennsylvania colony. Delaware remained part of Pennsylvania until the Revolutionary War. In 1787, the region, with its population of about 37,000, became a separate state.

> The colony, split into West Jersey and East Jersey, remained so until 1702, when the proprietors surrendered their rights and a united New Jersey became a royal colony.

James turned a large portion of New Jersey over to his friends Lord John Berkeley and Sir George Carteret. They provided for religious freedom for Protestants. Hundreds of Quakers, many of them artisans and shopkeepers, settled in the western part of the colony.

The New Jersey proprietorship shifted in 1673, with Carteret retaining the eastern part. Berkeley sold his rights to two Quakers—Edward Byllynge and John Fenwick. They, in turn, sold out to three other Quakers, one of whom was William Penn. The colony, split into West Jersey and East Jersey, remained so until 1702, when the proprietors surrendered their rights and a united New Jersey became a royal colony.

The Carolinas.

In 1629, King Charles I of England gave a huge area of land south of Virginia to Sir Robert Heath, naming the region *Province of Carolana*, meaning "land of Charles." (The spelling was changed to *Carolina* in 1663.) Heath made no effort to colonize, and in 1663 Charles II reissued the grant. This time it went to eight proprietors, one of whom was Sir William Berkeley, a former governor of Virginia.

Immigrants soon settled at Albemarle Point near what is now Charleston. They came from England, Virginia, and the island of Barbados in the West Indies, where the English had established vast sugar plantations.

Quaker James Fenwick settled on Salem Creek, in what is now the southwestern part of New Jersey. In 1682, Fenwick and his partners sold the settlement to three other Quakers, including William Penn.

In 1712, Carolina was formally split. South Carolina became a royal colony in 1719, and North Carolina became a royal colony in 1729.

By 1750, about 25,000 European settlers lived in South Carolina. Thirty years later, that population had risen to about 90,000. The population of North Carolina was then about 350,000.

Carolinians and Native Americans.

Apart from occasional minor conflicts, relations between the Indians and the settlers in the Carolinas remained friendly for a number of years. As in other colonies, European immigrants learned about "New World" agriculture from the Indians, and the Indians welcomed opportunities to exchange furs for manufactured goods, including guns.

The settlers' attitude toward the Indians, however, was much the same in the Carolinas as it was in most other colonies. As an early Carolina settler noted:

They always freely give us of their vituals at their quarters, while we let them walk by our doors hungry, and do not often relieve them. We look upon them with disdain and scorn, and think them little better than beasts. . . .

Relations between the two groups began to sour when the growing immigrant population began to encroach on Indian land, whether they purchased it or not. At the same time, the Indians became increasingly resentful of the fur traders' tendency to cheat them whenever possible. The result was war—the Tuscarora War in North Carolina and the Yamasee War to the south—which equaled, in ferocity and destruction, both the Pequot War in Connecticut and King Philip's War in New England.

The Tuscarora War.

In 1710, about 400 immigrants settled the community of New Bern. Their farms encroached on Tuscarora land, sometimes cutting off the Indians' access to the rivers.

At dawn on Sept. 22, 1711, an estimated 500 Tuscarora attacked New Bern, killing about 140 settlers. North Carolinians appealed to South Carolinians for help, and 33 settlers responded along with about 500 Yamasee Indians. In January 1712, the combined force destroyed Tuscarora villages and fields and attacked Tuscarora forts.

The Tuscarora made peace that spring, but the settlers captured some Tuscarora and sold them into slavery. This led to more Indian attacks in the summer and fall of 1712. Counterattacks by colonists resulted in 950 Indian men, women, and children being killed, wounded, or captured. Many of the Indian prisoners were forced into slavery. Some 22 settlers were killed and 36 were wounded. In 1715, the Tuscarora and the settlers finally made peace.

The Yamasee War.

Although the Yamasee of South Carolina had sided with the settlers in the Tuscarora War, the alliance was short-lived. The Yamasee had many of the same grievances against settlers as the Tuscarora did. The Yamasee War began on April 15, 1715, when bands of Yamasee attacked settlements near Beaufort. Other Indian tribes, including the Creek and Catawba, joined the Yamasee, but the Cherokee—ancient enemies of the Creek—chose to support the settlers.

Troops from Massachusetts, Virginia, North Carolina, and South Carolina all became involved in the Yamasee War. In the end, 400 settlers were dead or wounded, vast amounts of property had been destroyed, and a great deal of money had been expended. The war's outcome, though, was seemingly inevitable. By spring 1716, the Indians were thoroughly defeated.

Actually, if the various Indian tribes had been able to put aside their differences and unite, it is possible they might have driven the Europeans back into the sea. The Indian bow and arrow had several advantages over the European musket. Although an arrow did less damage than a soft-lead shot from a musket, it was more accurate over a longer distance and, in any event, it did enough harm to stop an attacker. In addition, an Indian could shoot from six to ten arrows in the time it took a European to shoulder a musket, fire, and reload. Since the locksmiths who repaired muskets worked only in port towns where there was enough business, many Europeans carried damaged muskets that seldom hit their target, and if it rained or snowed, the musket did not fire at all.

Wars between the Indians and the settlers were common events in the late 1600's and early 1700's. This crude woodcut from the era shows a group of Indians being attacked on two sides by settlers.

Life in most colonial homes centered around the fireplace. The women prepared food there, and cooking utensils hung nearby. The fireplace provided most of the family's heat and light, and everyone gathered in front of it to eat, work, or relax.

Georgia. In January 1733, a ship bearing James Oglethorpe and 114 immigrants bound for Georgia put in briefly at Charleston, S.C. Upon receiving news of the newcomers' arrival, the South Carolina government presented them with 100 cows, 5 bulls, 20 sows, and 4 boars.

The South Carolinians rejoiced at the prospect of a colony to the south. It would fulfill their desire for a defensive border against French fur-trading activity in what was then called the Alabama Country and against the Spanish in Florida. However, James Oglethorpe had his own reason for founding Georgia.

In 1728, Oglethorpe's friend Robert Castell went to prison for failure to pay debts, a common fate of English debtors at the time. In prison, Castell got smallpox and died. Oglethorpe then began an investigation of prison conditions and the poor treatment inmates received. His efforts led to the release of 10,000 debtors.

Spurred on by his success, Oglethorpe created a plan for a colony that would be a haven for debtors. In 1732, King George II granted a 21-year charter and land in North America to the Trustees for Establishing the Colony of Georgia—named after the king. By then, though, the colony's purpose had been changed, and the

land was designated for the poor. The English government's main interest, however, like that of the South Carolinians, lay in creating a colony for defense.

The original immigrants included perhaps a dozen debtors, but by the time the charter ran out, about half the 4,000 or so settlers in Georgia were poor immigrants whose expenses had been paid by the Trustees.

The reform element in the founding of Georgia carried over into some of the laws the Trustees issued. One such law was "for Suppressing the odious and loathsome Sin of Drunkenness." However, America's first attempt at prohibition met with no more success than did the nationwide experiment of the 1920's and 1930's.

Spain protested the colony's founding on the grounds that the land

Fishing was a major industry in the New England colonies. Major port cities were within easy sailing distance of the finest fishing waters in North America, including the area known as the Grand Banks, off the coast of New-foundland. Each year, huge amounts of herring, cod, hali-but, and mackerel were salted and dried for export. The best grades of fish were sold in Europe. The poorer grades were sold in the West Indies as food for the slaves on sugar plantations.

belonged to Spain. By the 1740's, England and Spain were at war, and Georgia received its first test as a defensive colony, but skirmishes over the next few years were inconclusive.

Trade with England. All in all, the thirteen English colonies met Richard Hakluyt's highest expectations and became sources of raw materials for England's industry and ready markets for England's manufactured goods. The colonists shipped a long list of items to England including turpentine and pine pitch, lumber, corn, fruit, rice, wheat, dried and salted fish, beaver pelts, tobacco, and ingredients for dyes such as indigo.

The colonists got many manufactured goods from England in return. These included kettles and other cooking utensils, fine furniture, tableware, clothing, tea, saws, hatchets, axes, guns, swords, shoe buckles, ribbon, brass clocks, and compasses.

The colonists made some of the things they needed, though, including simple clothing, furniture, and shoes. Skilled artisans in colonial towns and cities turned out more expensive and finely made clothing and shoes, as well as silverware and other articles. English law forbade the colonial manufacture of hats, fine woolens, and ironware, but those regulations were not strictly enforced. Merchants who dealt in overseas trade did a brisk business, as did shipbuilders at ports such as Boston. Despite these successes, though, the English generally profited more than the colonists who supplied them.

PART 5: EUROPEANS BECOME AMERICANS

The English colonies attracted tens of thousands of people during the 1700's and 1800's. By 1775, about 2.5 million people lived along the Atlantic seaboard, and they no longer thought of themselves as transplanted Europeans but as a new people—Americans.

By the middle of the 1700's, Boston was a bustling city of more than 12,000 people and had become the leading fishing and shipbuilding center of the colonies.

133

Visitors were always welcome at the luxurious plantations of the South. However, the same homes often employed tutors, such as the one depicted in the statue, who were noted for their stern approach.

CHAPTER 12: IRISH, SCOTS, GERMANS, JEWS, AND OTHERS

I mmigrants to the English colonies after the year 1630 came to a wilderness where establishing a new society exacted a heavy toll in physical labor, primitive living conditions, and wars with unfriendly Indians. Although they suffered much less than the unfortunate settlers who experienced Jamestown's terrible first years, there still was more than sufficient hardship.

The christening of a new baby or a quilting bee were good opportunities for colonial people to get together and socialize.

By the 1700's, aside from the ocean voyage, which remained perilous, much had changed. The frontier had been moved back from the sea. Some cleared land was available to those who could afford the higher price it fetched over wilderness acreage. A number of transportation routes were in place. The colonists had organized churches, governments, and other institutions. Sawmills turned out beams and clapboards for homes and shops, and there were mills for grinding grain. Newcomers no longer had to bring livestock with them. Cities such as Philadelphia and Boston were well established and growing. In addition to commercial and investment opportunities, they offered employment for both artisans and unskilled laborers.

While there was still room for pioneering, it was no longer the only option.

Economic betterment remained the main goal for many immigrants, and tens of thousands achieved that goal. Writing in 1743 from Georgia—then only a decade old and by no means the most prosperous colony—one John Bolzius reported:

> All industrious people live more comfortably here than in their native country and beg in their letters frequently that their relatives might follow them to this colony.

1770's, the colonial population included about 200,000 people of Irish descent.

Some immigrants paid their own way across the Atlantic. However, most were too poor to afford the passage. They became indentured servants, agreeing to work for a number of years to pay for the cost of their transportation.

The Scotch-Irish. Another important immigrant group were the Scotch-Irish, so-called because they

By 1776, some 250,000 Scotch-Irish lived in America. Most settled in the Middle Colonies, especially in Pennsylvania.

The Irish. Many of the immigrants to the colonies came from Ireland. Their reasons for migrating included escape from religious and political persecution.

English subjugation of Ireland began in the 1100's, under Henry II. It was formally established in 1541 when Henry VIII forced Ireland's parliament to declare him king of Ireland. The bitter Irish staged several revolts in the late 1500's and early 1600's, but the English put them down brutally.

By 1704, Catholics were forbidden to purchase, inherit, or even rent land. They could not serve in Parliament, and their religious practices were severely restricted.

Clearly, Catholics had plenty of reason to leave Ireland. Thousands of Irish Protestants also lived in poverty, and their reasons for migrating to America were equally strong. By the

were Scots who lived in Ireland. After rebellions in northern Ireland during the 1600's, the English government had opened the northern region called Ulster to settlement by Scots. By 1700, thousands of Scots lived in Ulster and had brought with them their Presbyterian religion. Within a few years, however, many left Ulster for the colonies. Despite religious persecution, their reasons for leaving were more economic than religious. Landlords renting to Scotch-Irish farmers frequently raised rents while spending little or nothing on the land to make it more valuable.

The Scotch-Irish woolen and linen industries suffered too. The Woolen Act of 1699 forbade Scotch-Irish weavers from exporting cloth to any country where it would compete with cloth manufactured in England.

By 1776, some 250,000 Scotch-Irish lived in America. Most settled in the Middle Colonies, especially in Pennsylvania.

The Scots. In the 1600's, a group of Scots convicted of rebellion against the Scottish government were shipped to America to serve out their prison terms. When they reached the colonies, they were sold to settlers as indentured servants. Most Scots, however, left their homeland voluntarily. Many settled in the Carolinas, Pennsylvania, and in the Mohawk Valley of New York. By 1790, about 260,000 colonists were Scottish immigrants or their descendants.

Life as an indentured servant—especially in the Middle Colonies—could be quite difficult. This was especially true in Maryland and Virginia. In the 1600's, the average life expectancy in Maryland and Virginia was 40 for men and 39 for women. At the same time, the average life expectancy in New England was 68. In fact, after 1680 most indentured servants were convicts because freemen wouldn't come.

The Germans and the Swiss. In the early 1700's, thousands of German-speaking Lutherans came to America. They fled from a devastating war in the Rhine Valley, very burdensome taxation, and an economic depression in Germany's wine-growing regions.

The Germans learned enough English to carry on commercial relationships with other colonists. However, they spoke German in their communities, published German-language newspapers and books, and conducted their religious services in German. They also maintained their own grammar schools, where pupils were taught in German.

Quaker artist Edward Hicks painted this scene of his childhood home of the late 1700's. Quakers believed that salvation lay in the "peaceable kingdom" of a serene and well-ordered heart. Hicks visualized this belief in spiritual landscapes crowded with animals that symbolize human vices and virtues. Hicks is best known for a series of paintings called The Peaceable Kingdom.

Soon there were inklings of a major continuing theme in American history—prejudice against whichever was the newest group of immigrants. Ben Franklin probably expressed the sentiments of many English-speaking colonists toward German exclusivity when he asked, in his *Observations on the Increase of Mankind and the Peopling of Countries*, published in 1751:

> Why should Pennsylvania, founded by the English, become a Colony of *Aliens*, who will shortly be so numerous as to Germanize us instead of our Anglifying them, and will never adopt our language?

Franklin believed that the Germans should be forced to mix with English settlers, that the children of German immigrants should attend English-language schools, and that all public documents should be printed in English only. He also thought that public office should be denied to anyone not speaking English. However, he insisted:

> I am not against the admission of Germans in general, for they have their virtues. Their industry and frugality are exemplary. They are excellent husbandmen [farmers] and contribute greatly to the improvement of a country.

That faint praise, however, failed to mollify German voters, whose ballots helped remove Franklin from his seat in the Assembly.

The Germans in Pennsylvania were known as *Pennsylvania Dutch*. The term came from the Old English word *Deutsch*, meaning German. Pennsylvania Dutch farmers were noted for their well-kept farms, their industriousness, the care they gave their livestock, and their huge barns.

Building barns was a community event among German settlers. After a farmer dug the foundation and prepared the rafters and other wooden

A colonial housewife's chores often involved making butter—sometimes with fancy butter molds as shown here—and butchering hogs.

Old mrs. Hausman Killing a Hog and a beef for me. Dr. John Rouse in 1802. her general practice

This hand-drawn birth and baptismal certificate is a good example of Pennsylvania Dutch folk art of the era. It also shows the love and devotion of parents toward a new child. At the time, many children died in infancy. The ones who survived were often especially treasured.

parts, he invited his neighbors over to help raise the barn. While the men worked at their task, the women set the dinner table with all sorts of delicacies, ranging from metzel soup and hamburg sausage to apple pies and cider. The day ended with everyone dancing on the new barn's threshing floor.

The **Jews.** The first Jewish immigrants arrived on a French ship that docked at New Amsterdam in 1654. The group consisted of 4 men, 6 women, and 13 children. They had come from Brazil.

New Amsterdam Dutch, led by Governor Peter Stuyvesant, were not pleased at the Jews' arrival. A Dutch clergyman bemoaned the presence in the colony of Catholics, Protestants, even atheists—and now came Jews to further add to the religious confusion.

The Dutch West India Company—which had a number of Jewish stockholders—ordered that the newcomers from Brazil be allowed to remain. Colonial authorities, however, refused to give the Jewish immigrants permission to establish a synagogue, would not allow them the vote, and forbade them to own land or trade with the Indians. When the British took over New Netherland in 1664, they removed most of these restraints. However, Jews were not allowed to start construction of a synagogue until 1728.

Despite these limitations, the Jews moved to establish themselves in their new home. They formed Congregation Shearith Israel, meaning Remnant of Israel, and conducted religious services in one another's homes.

When Stuyvesant ruled that Jews could not stand guard duty with Christians but had to pay a tax instead, a strong-willed young man

Built in 1763, the Touro Synagogue in Newport, R.I., is the oldest one in America today.

American banker and patriot Haym Salomon was a Polish Jew who arrived in 1772 and soon became involved in the Revolutionary War. The British arrested him twice as a spy. The second time, he was sentenced to death but escaped by bribing his jailer. He made many loans to the American army and government. His sudden death in 1785 meant that the money was never repaid.

named Asher Levy objected. He refused to pay the tax, insisting that he was physically fit to help protect the colony, and eventually won his point. He also won the right to open a butcher's shop. Soon, Jews were allowed to enter the lucrative fur trade with the Indians.

Between 2,000 and 3,000 Jews had settled in the colonies by the time of the Revolutionary War, establishing congregations in port cities such as Newport, R.I.; Philadelphia; Charleston; and Savannah; as well as New York. Many became prominent in business and commerce. For example, the well-known Hendricks family

St. Bartholomew's Day Massacre of 1572. Finally, in 1598, the Edict of Nantes gave the Huguenots the same civil rights as French Catholics and allowed them to practice their religion. Nearly 100 years later, however, in 1685, Louis XIV revoked the Edict of Nantes, once more opening the gate to persecution of the Huguenots. As a result, about 14,000 fled to the English colonies.

Immigration Restrictions and Citizenship. The Puritan ideal in Massachusetts included religious uni-

---

Between 2,000 and 3,000 Jews had settled in the colonies by the time of the Revolutionary War.

---

opened the first copper mill in the colonies with ore obtained from mines in New Jersey. The Jews of Newport developed much of the colonial whaling industry, as well as the manufacture of soap and candles from whale oil. Members of the Gratz family of Philadelphia and the Gomez family of New York were active in trade along the Atlantic coast and in the West Indies. Haym Salomon, who achieved wealth as a financier, aided the revolutionary cause by raising large amounts of money through bond issues and by equipping entire military units from his own funds.

The Huguenots. The Huguenots were French Protestants. During the 1500's, they made up about one sixth of the population of France. In 1562, a civil war broke out between Catholic and Protestant nobles who were competing for the throne. During the course of the war, some 10,000 Huguenots were killed in the notorious

formity and ethnic homogeneity. In Massachusetts and elsewhere, however, the main objection to unrestricted immigration had to do with taxes.

Communities were expected to take care of their poor, and the influx of many poverty-stricken immigrants strained available resources. According to one source, Boston's cost of caring for the poor was five times higher in 1737 than it had been just 10 years earlier. Local authorities began requiring sea captains to guarantee that the immigrants they unloaded would not become public charges. However, hundreds of Scotch-Irish who landed in Boston went from the ship to the workhouse because they were unable to support themselves. On one occasion in the 1720's, an angry mob tried to prevent a shipload of Scotch-Irish from disembarking.

To make British citizens of immigrants who came from outside the British Isles, colonial governments began issuing deeds of "denization." As preliminary to full citizenship,

By the end of the 1700's, more and more families were starting off for what was then the West—Pittsburgh. The long, slow trip through western Pennsylvania often took three months to complete.

these deeds granted the immigrants certain privileges, including the right to own property. However, the British government was not obligated to honor the deeds. Parliament finally passed a naturalization law for the colonies in 1740, offering British citizenship to any individual who had lived on British territory continuously for seven years.

Labor Shortage.

A shortage of labor, which drove up wages, characterized much of the colonial period. A major reason for this labor shortage was the availability of land, particularly during the first century or so of colonization. Whenever they could manage it, colonists tried to acquire land and strike out for themselves rather than work for someone else.

As early as the 1630's, settlers in Massachusetts Bay were complaining about the lack of reliable workers to help with farm chores and household tasks. They also complained about the high wages they had to pay. For example, an unskilled laborer was paid about twice as much money in New England as in England. Skilled workers did even better.

Learning about America.

Colonial governments actively recruited immigrants, often by playing on the desire for land ownership. In 1619 for example, Virginia set up the so-called headright system, under which a person already living in the colony could obtain 50 acres (20 hectares) by paying a new immigrant's passage to America.

However, the headright system greatly benefited speculators and a few wealthy Virginia merchants who sold their land grants, either to other colonists or to new immigrants. As a result, Virginia changed the program in 1705, relying instead on direct government land sales at low prices. Maryland and the Carolinas followed the same practice.

Such proprietors as William Penn, Lord Calvert, and Anthony Ashley Cooper of Carolina advertised their colonies in European newspapers. In some instances, the proprietors reached into their own pockets to pay the immigrants' transportation costs and furnish them with equipment to get started in America. Penn was the most active recruiter of all. He not only flooded Europe with pamphlets and broadsides extolling Pennsylvania's virtues but also traveled to Europe himself to publicize his colony and oversee recruitment.

Many Germans learned about America from agents called "newlanders." These individuals contracted with merchants or sea captains to provide candidates for immigration at a specific price per head. Well dressed, and frequently posing as merchants, newlanders ranged the Rhine Valley spinning wondrous tales of life in America where—they assured their listeners—anyone could live like a noble.

Newlanders appealed mostly to landless peasants and unemployed farm laborers—individuals with very little money. However, after paying the cost of transportation to an immigrant port, many of them were broke. Since there was no turning back, they then had to agree to accept indentured servitude to pay their passage to America. The profit went to the merchants and ship captains who sponsored them.

In England, thousands of men and women heard about America from a judge as he said the words "transportation to the colonies" as the sentence pronounced after a criminal trial. Although English prisons were wretched, transportation was not much better. About 15 per cent died aboard ship. Sea captains who transported criminals sold them into indentured servitude at dockside in the colonies for the price of passage—plus profit. In the Middle Colonies, many indentured servants were literally worked to death. Before 1690, indentured servants were a cheaper form of labor than slaves and were always potential future competition.

In 1751, replying to English arguments favoring transportation, Benjamin Franklin asked if colonials would be justified in sending their rattlesnakes to England. However, it should not be assumed that all transported criminals were either murderers or rapists. Some were juvenile delinquents, others were guilty of nothing more than simple trespass or stealing a loaf of bread. Furthermore, the English government often transported Scottish and Irish political prisoners.

In any case, the colonials continued to protest the transportation system, and the English government continued to use the system. Out of almost 50,000 transportees who arrived in America during the colonial period, an estimated 20,000 landed in Maryland alone, where they were known as "seven-year" or "king's" passengers.

Colonial proprietors such as William Penn sometimes advertised their enterprises on sets of playing cards that were sold in Europe in the hope that the ads would encourage people to emigrate. These two cards show people purchasing land and then clearing it for farming. The use of pictures along with words helped get the point across to anyone who might not be able to read—a common fate in those days.

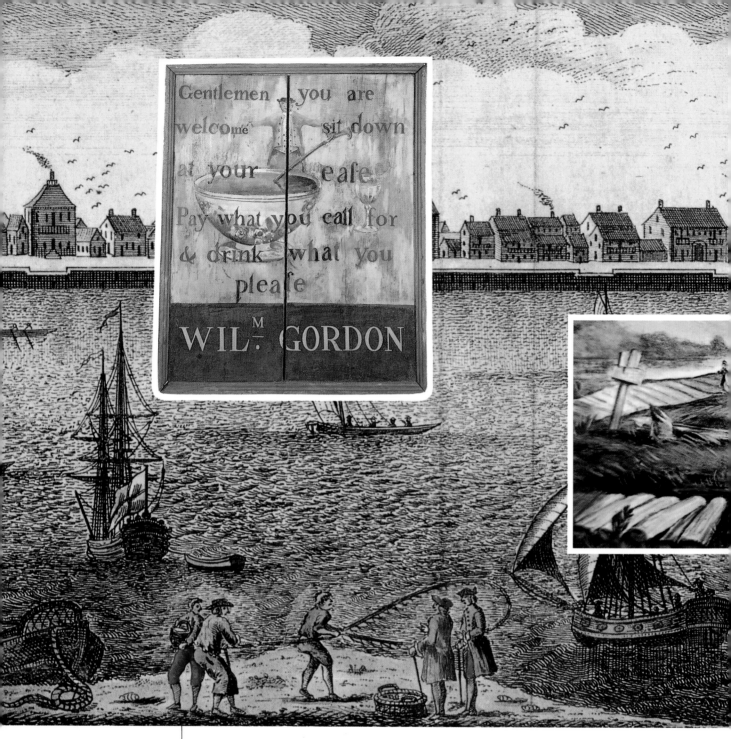

By 1762, Charleston, S.C., was a thriving seaport, as shown here, and its people kept in contact with other colonists through the new mail system. In 1753, Philadelphian Ben Franklin had been named deputy postmaster general of the colonies. He improved the frequency and reliability of mail deliveries.

CHAPTER 13: THE ATLANTIC CROSSING AND BEYOND

For many immigrants, the greatest barrier to a better life in America was the ocean crossing. Long delays were common while ships were made ready at English seaports and at Amsterdam and Rotterdam in the Netherlands. Once at sea, an Atlantic crossing under favorable circumstances usually took 8 to 10 weeks. On the other hand, some voyages—because of storms and adverse winds, accidents, and even pirate attacks—lasted as long as six months.

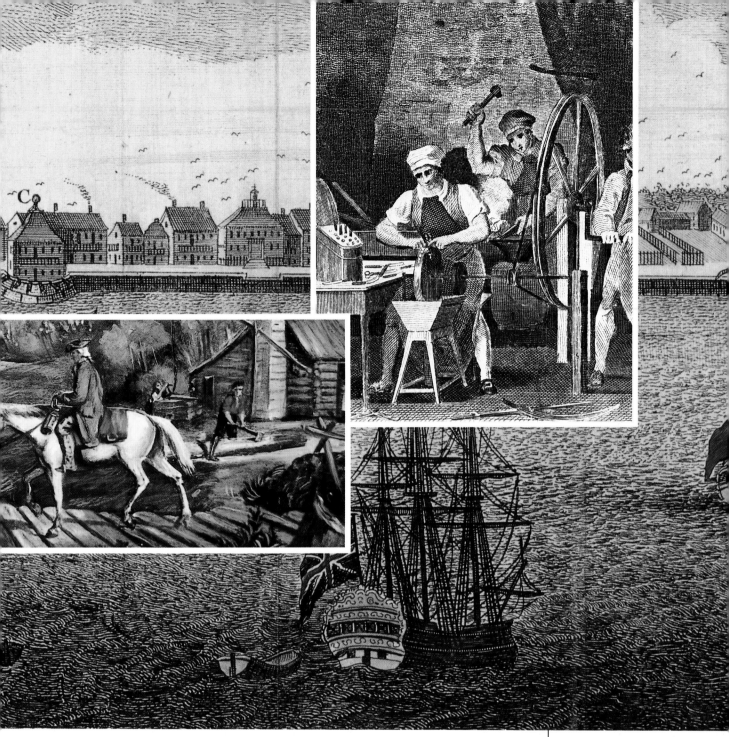

Life aboard the typical sailing ship was cramped and uncomfortable at best, miserable and dangerous at worst. As many as 300 people were jammed between decks with space allotments of about 6 feet (1.8 meters) per person. Privacy was nonexistent, as were laundry facilities. Several weeks of wearing the same clothing—without taking a bath—undoubtedly produced overwhelming odors.

Rations on board ship consisted of items such as dried vegetables, dried beef, salted fish, hard biscuits, butter—or what passed for butter—beer, and water. There was not always enough to provide three meals a day, and the longer the voyage, the less wholesome the food became. Biscuits turned into meals for red worms, butter and drinking water became rancid, and beer soured. In some cases, food

Colonists everywhere engaged in many types of work and relaxation. In the numerous taverns, people often gathered to eat, drink, gossip, and play cards. Colonial businesses included those that made and repaired knives and scissors.

ran out entirely, leaving passengers to chew on scraps of old leather and on rats and mice they managed to catch.

Storms and cold weather often forced passengers to remain below deck for long periods of time. Lice were familiar companions, and disease was a constant threat. Scurvy, smallpox, and dysentery were especially widespread. Disease hit children especially hard, and few under the age of seven survived the voyage. One passenger recalled seeing the bodies of 32 children thrown overboard during the journey.

Indentured Servitude. It has been estimated that during the colonial period, more than half the almost 1 mil-

that specified what the indentured servant would receive at the end of the indenture term. For example:

> Eva Wagner with consent of her father to John M. Brown of Northern Libertyes, Philadelphia County, Riger, for five years, to have six months' schooling and at the end of the term two complete suits of clothes, one of which to be new, also one Straw bed, one bedstead, one Blanket, one pillow and one sheet.

So-called soul-drivers purchased indentured servants wholesale from captains, then paraded them from town to town, selling them to the highest bidder. Indenture auctions at dockside, whether by captains or soul-drivers, were common.

Indentured servants were not paid wages during the indenture term. Instead, they received food, clothing, and shelter.

lion immigrants paid for their passage by working as indentured servants. They signed contracts of indenture before they boarded ship or after they arrived. Transported criminals were forcibly indentured.

An indentured servant agreed to work for a period of years—usually four, sometimes seven—for a person who paid the passage to America. Indentured servants under 5 years of age were required to serve until age 21. However, most indentured servants were young men between the ages of 15 and 25. Although a few were artisans, most of the young men were unskilled farm laborers.

Indentured servants were not paid wages during the indenture term. Instead, they received food, clothing, and shelter. Indenture contracts also spelled out so-called freedom dues

Laws protected indentured servants, and they could bring suit if their masters did not fulfill the contract terms, deprived them of medical attention, or mistreated them. Indentured servants could also sue to obtain their freedom dues. In the area known as the Chesapeake, the court judges were usually the plantation owners themselves, so few suits were ever brought there.

On the other hand, indentured servants were considered part of an estate and could be seized to satisfy a master's debt or be bequeathed. For example, Rebecca Royston, a widow, left an estate that included "1 servant boy 8 years to serve."

Indentured servants could be punished—often by a whipping—for shirking duties and for disobeying their master. They could not buy liq-

THIS INDENTURE witnesseth, that JOHN NEMO, by the Consent of : : : : hath put himself, and by these Presents, with the Consent aforesaid, doth Voluntarily, and of his own free Will and Accord, put himself Apprentice to Philip Sharp of Bristol, to learn his Art, Trade and Mystery, and after the Manner of an Apprentice to serve him, his Executors and Assigns from the Day of the Date hereof, for, & during, & to the full End & Term, of (die Jahre) next ensuing: During all which Term, the said Apprentice his said Master faithfully shall serve, his Secrets keep, his lawful Commands every where readily obey. He shall do no Damage to his said Master nor see it to be done by others, without letting or giving Notice thereof to his said Master, he shall not waste his said Masters Goods, nor lend them unlawfully to any. He shall not commit Fornication, nor contract Matrimony, within the said Term: At Cards, Dice, or any other unlawful Games he shall not play, whereby his said Master may have Damage. With his own Goods, nor the Goods of others, without Licence from his said Master, he shall neither buy nor sell. He shall not absent himself Day nor Night from his said Masters Service without his Leave: Nor haunt Ale-houses, Taverns, or Play-houses; but in all Things behave himself as a faithful Apprentice ought to do, during the said Term. And the said Master shall use the utmost of his Endeavour to teach, or cause to be taught and instructed the said Apprentice in the Trade or Mystery of a Taylor, and procure and provide for him sufficient Meat, Drink, Apparel, Lodging and Washing, fitting for an Apprentice, during the said Term of : : : YEARS

uor, nor marry without their master's consent. Nor could they vote or hold office.

Although the law provided for severe punishment such as whipping and longer terms for those who ran away, a good many did. One historian counted 110 advertisements for runaways in the *Virginia Gazette* alone between 1736 and 1739. A typical ad ran like this:

Run away about Two Years ago from Cecil County in Maryland, Nicholas Collings, small Stature, bushy Hair almost Grey: A Shoemaker by Trade. Whoever secures him, and gives Notice thereof to Mr. Abel van Burkeloo of the said County, shall have Ten Shillings Reward.

Another ad spoke of Nancy Perron, who ran away from one James Willson. It described her as having a round face and an impudent look.

Since nothing distinguished an indentured servant from any other colonist, runaways probably found it fairly easy to melt into city populations or disappear on the frontier.

Some were caught, however, as this ad in the *Pennsylvania Gazette* in 1760 attests:

Taken up and committed to Lancaster gaol, one Henry Reigdurff, lately advertised for running away from one John Chamber, of Birmingham Township, Chester County: These are to require said John Chamber, or others whom it may concern, to come and take him out and pay the charges to the gaoler.

Travel to and life in the colonies could be difficult. A sailor named Ashley Brown drew his ship Swift *in a storm during a trip to Boston in 1741. Contracts for indentures were often long and precise. This one forbids the servant to marry, play dice, or go to plays.*

Summing up the great value of those hundreds of thousands of immigrants who worked under contract, Benjamin Franklin wrote in 1759:

> The labor of the plantations [colonies] is performed chiefly by indentured servants brought from Great Britain, Ireland, and Germany, because the high price it bears cannot be performed in any other way.

Once indentured servants received their freedom, they had the option of working for wages, establishing a trade or business, or acquiring land of their own. It has been estimated that perhaps 1 in 10 succeeded in becoming landowners. The rest, being generally unskilled, worked mostly as laborers and tenant farmers.

However, a few former indentured servants achieved considerable success. For example, Charles Thomson—who was secretary of the Continental Congress in the 1770's—and Matthew Thornton and George Taylor—who signed the Declaration of Independence—all began life in the colonies as indentured servants. So did Daniel Dulany, a prominent Maryland lawyer.

Some women rose from the humble status of indentured servant through marriage. For example, Mary Morril, Benjamin Franklin's maternal grandmother, married her master, Peter Folger. Eleanor Stevenson, a servant of Sir Edmund Plowden, later married William Branthwaite, deputy governor of Maryland.

Indentured servitude persisted throughout the colonial period. It eventually ended in the early 1800's.

Social Classes. Social stratification was the norm in the countries from which indentured servants and other immigrants came. A similar sys-

Even as dissatisfaction with English rule grew, most things English remained the fashion in colonial America. This included clothing styles, furniture, and recreation. Wealthy colonists, especially in the Middle Colonies, liked to indulge in the popular English sport of fox hunting.

tem developed in the colonies, and most colonists approved of it. However, there were some important differences. For one thing, no noble class developed in America. For another, social position in America was based not on birth, as in Europe, but on wealth. Also, the American system allowed for some social mobility—a son could achieve higher status than his father had enjoyed. However, since inherited land was a major source of wealth, social status was determined by ancestry in some ways.

Differences in forms of address as well as wealth identified social groups. For example, farmers were usually referred to as "the middling sort." They, along with members of the lower class in villages and cities, were usually addressed as "goodman." A man designated a "gentleman" was a man of means. A man placing *Esq.* after his name had higher rank.

As in Europe, members of the lower class in the colonies were expected to look up to and respect members of the upper class. They were also expected to dress differently from "their betters." Sumptuary laws prohibited "men and women of mean condition" from taking on "the garb of gentlemen, by wearing gold and silver lace, or buttons."

Such restrictions, however, did not mean that members of the lower class wore dark colors only. Quite the contrary. Although a person's "Sunday best" clothes were usually made from dark material, everyday clothes —at least along the Atlantic seaboard—were usually colored a bright red, russet, yellow, blue, or green. Men wore a linen shirt under a close-fitting jacket, breeches that came down below the knee, long stockings, and either moccasins or leather boots that laced up the front. Women wore

Large plantations in tidewater Virginia often looked like this one. It included a large, elaborate house for the owner and his family, much smaller homes for his employees, slave-quarters, ware-houses, and perhaps a schoolhouse for the owner's children. Being near a large navigable river was also important. It allowed the crops to be transported in the fastest, most eco-nomical manner. Travel by road was slow and often filled with problems in-cluding washed-out bridges, bandits, and broken wagon wheels.

a three-part outfit consisting of a skirt, a fitted waist, and a pair of sleeves that were tied around the arms. Depending on the weather, people wore one to five undergarments.

In the back country, although buckskin was easy and cheap to obtain, people along the frontier preferred to wear linen tops and woolen breeches and skirts. The reason was that when buckskin gets wet, it takes a long time to dry. During the process, the buckskin garment must be worn or it will lose its shape. All this can be very uncomfortable.

Social Successes. Among the early immigrants to Virginia were a few sons of the nobility and members of the English upper class. For exam-

ple, George Percy was the son of the Earl of Northumberland. By the 1700's, however, few middle- or high-born English remained in Virginia. The aristocracy was for the most part home-grown.

William Byrd of Westover, the third of his line in Virginia, was one example. The first William Byrd arrived in the colony in about 1670 to claim an inheritance of some 200 acres (80 hectares) from an uncle on his mother's side. He added to the estate and left William Byrd II comfortably well off. He, in turn, accumulated more, leaving William Byrd III more than 180,000 acres (72,000 hectares) of land as well as other resources. Members of the Byrd family remained prominent in Virginia politics and society for more than 300 years.

Women. In colonial times, marriage was encouraged to help increase the overall population. In the 1600's, people in New England usually married in their 20's. In the Chesapeake at the same time, girls often married as young as 13. By the 1700's, things had averaged out all over to a usual marriage age of 28 for men and 22 for women. In the 1600's—especially in Maryland and Virginia—male colonists outnumbered female six to one, so many early male settlers never found wives.

In general, the birth rate was high in the colonies, as it was everywhere in the world at that time. This was because children were considered an economic asset, especially on farms. However, the death rate was also high. Often, fewer than half the children born reached maturity. Many women, weakened by hard work and malaria, died in childbirth.

Wedlock at that time meant literally a "locking-in" of wife to husband. A woman could not, of course, vote. Furthermore, she was expected to be an "obedient wife," and her husband could legally inflict corporal punishment on her.

Since wives were usually younger than their husbands, those who survived childbirth usually ended up as widows. Widows who remarried often demanded premarriage contracts that guaranteed their continued control over the property they brought to the marriage. All colonies also honored dower rights, which guaranteed a widow the use of a third of all her late husband's property during her lifetime. In part, this guarantee kept widows off the public dole. Widows frequently carried on their late husbands' businesses, toiling as alehouse keepers, printers, shopkeepers, innkeepers, tanners, gunsmiths, and, in some instances, as lawyers. Many women worked as midwives.

Women practiced medicine as well as midwifery. They received no training, but then, neither did most male doctors—it was a matter of learning while doing.

Colonial doctors made considerable use of plants in their work. They prescribed lemon juice to prevent scurvy and recommended sassafras tea to cure the liver. They made the gum of the white poplar tree into an ointment that would "heale any green wound." They used tobacco to cure hangovers and applied a mixture of hot corn, milk, and fat to the jaw to relieve a toothache that was accompanied by swelling.

Colonial women also ran schools and served as private tutors. Martha Logan, in addition to boarding and teaching children in her home, managed a plantation 10 miles (16 kilometers) outside Charleston, S.C. Mary Willing Byrd, the second wife and widow of William Byrd III, took over the Byrd holdings upon his death and managed them well, in addition to rearing and educating eight children. By and large though, colonial life for women—and for men—was often short and harsh by today's standards. Only the hardiest individuals survived for long.

Elizabeth Timothy became the first woman newspaper editor and publisher in America when she continued the South Carolina Gazette in 1738 after the death of her husband, Lewis.

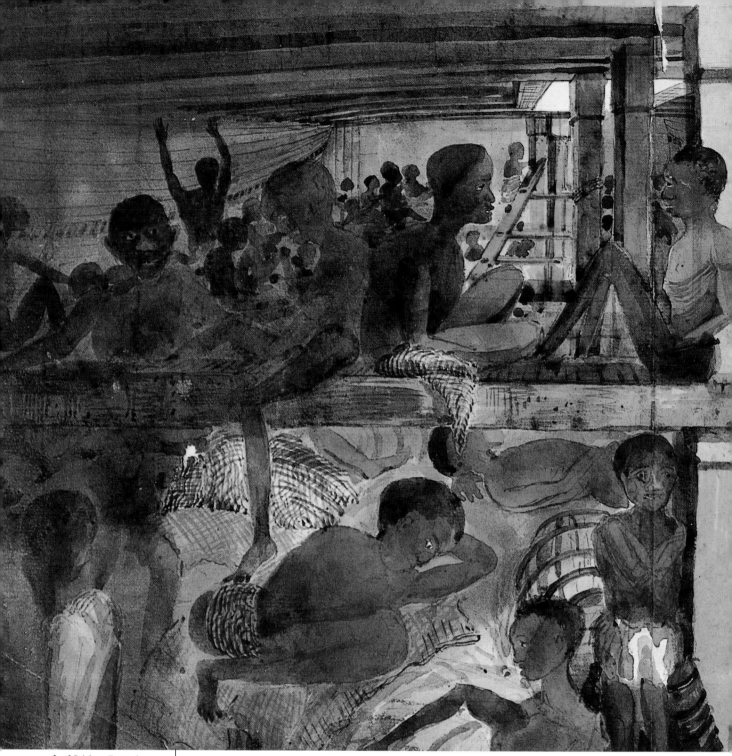

CHAPTER 14: IMMIGRANTS IN BONDAGE

lthough indentured servants in the English colonies worked in bondage, they could at least look forward to eventual freedom. However, this was not the case with another group of immigrants. The history of most people of African descent during colonial times and for many decades after was one of slavery and the horrors it entailed.

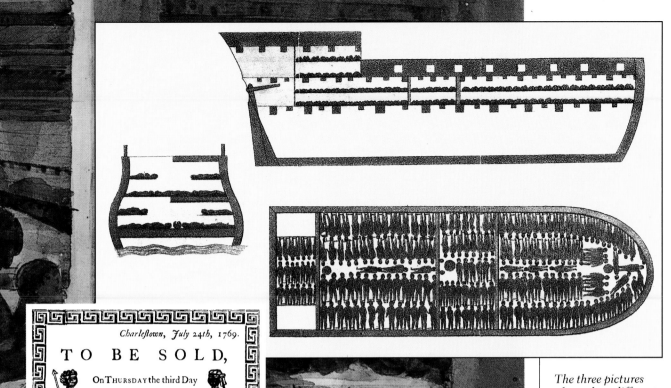

The three pictures above show different views of the living space for Africans on one slave ship. The voyages of such ships came to be called the middle passage, since the voyages made up the second part of a three-part process. In the first part, people were rounded up in Africa and sent to the Atlantic coast. In the second part, they traveled by ship to the Western Hemisphere. In the third part, they were sold at auction and taken to their new master's home. The auctions were often advertised with posters such as this one.

John Rolfe, the person who made to-bacco growing profitable in Virginia, recorded the arrival of the first Africans there in 1619: "About the last of August came in a dutch man of warre that sold us twenty Negars." More came in the years that followed, and a report in 1649 estimated that 300 of Virginia's population of 15,000 were Africans.

There is not enough evidence to determine the exact status of African Americans in the English colonies during those early years. Beginning in 1640, Virginia court records tell of sales of blacks "for their Life tyme" and, in the case of women, "and all their issue both male and female." A Virginia court dealt with three recovered runaway servants by sentencing two of them, both white, to an additional year of service. The third, an African American, was sentenced to "serve his said master or his assigns [heirs] for the time of his natural life here or elsewhere."

Sales of blacks for life and the right of owners to bequeath them to heirs were also recorded in Virginia and Maryland in the 1640's. Inventories of estates valued white servants in pounds of tobacco and with a specified number of years yet to serve. However, black servants were valued solely in terms of tobacco.

It is not difficult to figure out why colonists who needed workers preferred black slaves to white indentured servants. Slaves provided a lifetime of labor, and their offspring increased the work force. Aside from the initial

were wrenched from their homeland, family, and kinfolk—everything that was familiar to them—to live in an alien land among people with a lighter skin color who firmly believed in their cultural and religious superiority over blacks because of it.

Slave traders obtained their cargoes from local rulers along the west African coast. The Europeans and Americans offered such goods as iron, cloth, and especially guns in exchange. As the demand for overseas slaves increased, several African kingdoms—such as Benin, Dahomey, and the Ashanti Union—began to wage wars for the express purpose of obtaining slaves for sale. The result was not only political chaos in parts of west Africa but also the depopulation of large areas. Historians estimate that

Historians estimate that about 10 million Africans were brought to the Americas as slaves and that of this number, about 600,000 were shipped to North America.

price, it cost no more to provide food, clothing, and shelter for a slave than it did for an indentured servant. An African American's color made it difficult for a runaway to melt into the general population. Plantation owners in particular needed large gangs of laborers to tend their sugar cane, indigo, rice, and tobacco fields—and free white workers were reluctant to hire themselves out for such work.

Africans were familiar with the idea of slavery. For many years, they had enslaved those whom they captured in intertribal wars. Also, children were sometimes sold to pay a debt or to ensure the survival of the group in time of famine. With the coming of whites from overseas, however, slavery took on a different cast. For one thing, its purpose was strictly economic. It also meant that Africans

about 10 million Africans were brought to the Americas as slaves and that of this number, about 600,000 were shipped to North America.

At ports along the west African coast, Africans were herded aboard slave ships holding 400 or more. They were literally stacked between decks in spaces measuring 6 feet (1.8 meters) long and as little as 16 inches (40 centimeters) wide. Headroom often amounted to little more than 2 feet (60 centimeters) making it impossible even to sit upright, let alone stand. Toilet facilities were often just open tubs. In good weather, slaves were brought on deck and forced to exercise. In bad weather, they remained below.

Smallpox and other diseases took a dreadful toll. One European recorded the aftermath of a sweep of

THE TRIANGULAR TRADE

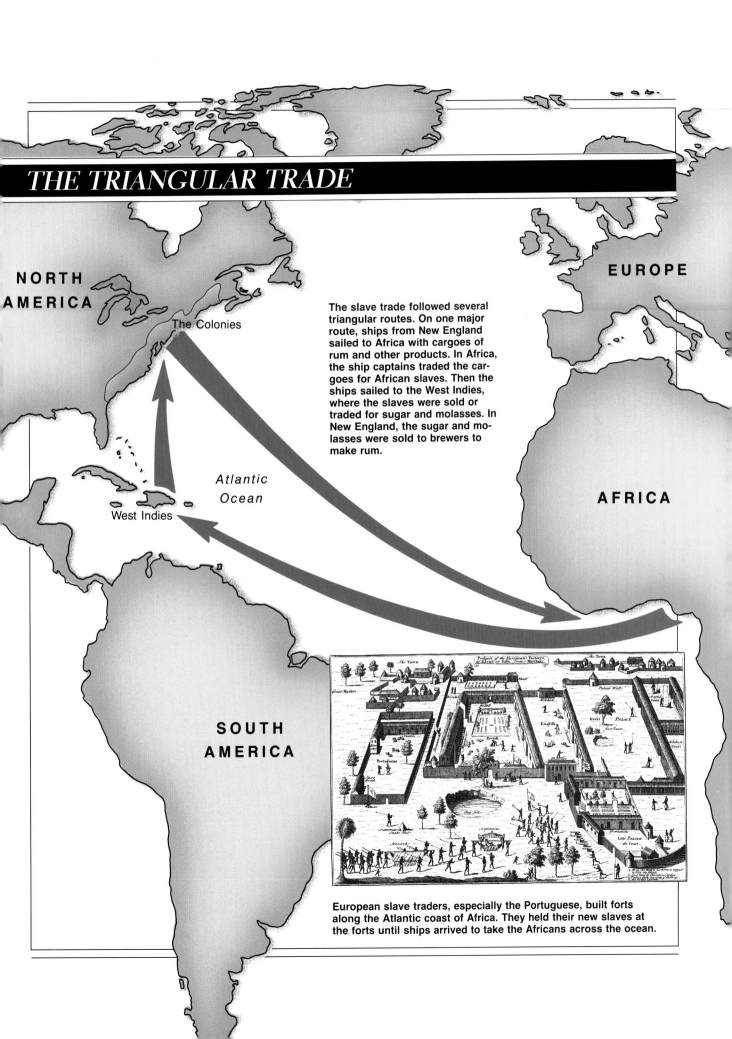

NORTH AMERICA

The Colonies

EUROPE

The slave trade followed several triangular routes. On one major route, ships from New England sailed to Africa with cargoes of rum and other products. In Africa, the ship captains traded the cargoes for African slaves. Then the ships sailed to the West Indies, where the slaves were sold or traded for sugar and molasses. In New England, the sugar and molasses were sold to brewers to make rum.

Atlantic Ocean

West Indies

AFRICA

SOUTH AMERICA

European slave traders, especially the Portuguese, built forts along the Atlantic coast of Africa. They held their new slaves at the forts until ships arrived to take the Africans across the ocean.

In the 1740's, plantations in South Carolina and elsewhere began growing indigo plants. When harvested, the plants were used to make a deep blue cloth dye that was very popular in England. Plantation slaves were usually used to harvest the crop and make the dye.

dysentery through slave quarters: "The floor of their rooms, was so covered with the blood and mucus which had proceeded from them in consequence of the flux, that it resembled a slaughterhouse." Suicides added to the death lists. Overall, about one in seven slaves died during transportation.

Slave ships either unloaded their human cargoes in the West Indies for transshipment to the English colonies or proceeded directly to such colonial ports as Charleston and New York City. In the colonies, ship captains negotiated individually with those who wished to buy slaves or else disposed of their cargoes at auction.

Slavery in Southern Colonies.

Slavery became a prominent feature in colonies such as Virginia and South Carolina where plantation economies developed. There, most blacks worked as field hands. Some performed household chores or became skilled blacksmiths, carpenters, or barrel makers.

For a time, Georgia was an exception to this pattern. James Oglethorpe and the Trustees of Georgia prohibited slavery in the colony in 1735. They believed slavery would defeat the colony's purposes of giving poor people a fresh start and of forming a defense against the Spaniards. They were convinced that having slaves would simply make colonists lazy. Many colonists disagreed with the Trustees, however, and arguments over slavery went on for several years. Those who favored slavery insisted that whites were unsuited for field work in the humid Southern climate. Opponents of slavery countered with examples of the abundant rice harvests that whites in Georgia had produced. In the meantime, more and more Georgians brought in more and more slaves from South Carolina. Finally, in 1750, the Trustees legalized reality by repealing the 1735 law.

By 1750, the Southern Colonies contained about 160,000 slaves, at least half of whom had been born there. About 88 per cent of slaveowners—those with small farms—owned only 2 or 3 slaves apiece. More than half the slaves in the South belonged to 12 per cent of the slaveowners and worked on plantations containing 20 or more slaves.

Slavery in Northern Colonies. The small-farm economy of Massachusetts did not lend itself to slavery. Most slaves in the colony were household servants in Boston. However, the economy was still linked to slaves through the businesses of shipbuilding, the manning of the ships, and slave transportation. Massachusetts merchants and sea captains engaged in the slave trade at least as early as 1645. Over approximately the next 150 years, New England sea captains and merchants continued to deposit the bulk of their slave cargoes in the West Indies or in Southern Colonies.

The first slaves, about 150 in all, arrived in Philadelphia three years after Pennsylvania was founded. William Penn himself became a slaveowner. By 1760, the city had about 1,000 African Americans working as artisans, day laborers, and household servants. There were only a few slaves in rural areas of Pennsyl-

vania. Many Quakers opposed slavery, however, and gradually convinced Pennsylvania's slaveowners to free their slaves. By the end of the colonial period, nearly 3,800 blacks remained in slavery in Pennsylvania, while about 6,500 had been freed. In 1790, Delaware recorded nearly 8,900 slaves and about 3,900 free blacks. Some 11,000 blacks, most of them slaves, lived in New Jersey at the time of the American Revolution.

New York had a larger African-American population than any other northern colony. The 1790 census counted 21,324 slaves there, along with 4,654 free blacks. Many New York slaveholders owned a few slaves at most. In New York City, as in Philadelphia and other cities, many owners hired out their slaves as menial or skilled laborers by the day or the week. Those doing the hiring were responsible for the slaves' room and board as well as their "rental fee."

In New York City, the rental price for skilled slaves rose 12 times over be-

In 1750, this picture appeared in a London magazine to show readers how tobacco was processed in Virginia.

tween 1695 and 1760. Nevertheless, even including the cost of food, clothing, and shelter, it was cheaper to hire skilled slaves than to employ white laborers. The latter angrily protested the competition from slaves, as Governor George Clarke reported concerning white coopers in 1737:

> The artificers complain and with too much reason of the pernicious [destructive] custom of breeding slaves to trades whereby the honest and industrious tradesmen are reduced to poverty for want of employ, and many of them forced to leave us to seek their living in other countries.

Resistance. An unrecorded number of African Americans resisted slavery by slowing down on the job to avoid exhaustion, performing shoddy work, or escaping. Some escapees found new homes among the Indians, but it was a dangerous game. Owners usually expended great effort to recover their "property." Blacks who seemed out of place were always subject to suspicion and to questioning and apprehension by the law. Once recaptured, an escapee was usually flogged, at least.

In 1712, a slave revolt broke out in New York City. A group of men only recently imported from Africa decided to strike a blow for freedom. They managed to obtain guns, swords, hatchets, and knives, and just after midnight on April 7, they went into action. One, named Coffee, set fire to a building. When whites came out, the rebels opened fire, killing five and wounding six. The whites rallied and drove the slaves into the woods. Sentries were posted to prevent the slaves from escaping, and without food and water, the rebels finally had to give up. Authorities then arrested 70 blacks who had taken part in the uprising or were suspected as accomplices and put them on trial. Much of the evidence presented at the trials was flimsy, and a number of blacks were unjustly convicted. The governor of New York ordered some cases dismissed, but in the end, 21 blacks were executed by being burned at the stake or broken on the rack and then hanged in chains.

Several years later, a slave uprising occurred in South Carolina. There, early in September 1739, about 20 blacks led by a slave named Jemmy raided a store in a small community south of Charleston. They killed the store owners, seized guns and powder, and began to lay waste the countryside.

That night, the rebels camped in a field. Beating drums, they attracted more slaves until their numbers grew to perhaps 100. They also gained the attention of the militia that had been called out. The subsequent battle did not last long. Militia guns cut down 14 blacks, and most of the remainder were captured. The majority were executed on the spot.

Benjamin Henry Latrobe was an opponent of slavery. In 1798, he painted this picture of slave women working in the fields while the white male overseer loafs nearby, smoking his pipe. Latrobe called his picture An Overseer Doing His Duty.

More than two dozen African Americans escaped, however, and set out for St. Augustine, Fla., which was then under Spanish rule. Some probably reached the Spanish town, but most were killed along the way in another encounter with the South Carolina militia. Altogether, the rebellion brought death to more than 20 whites and an uncounted number of African Americans.

The militia that put down these slave uprisings differed from the militia in England. There, only the richest men in the county could afford to equip themselves with the necessary heavy musket, ball and shot, long pike, sword, and brightly colored uniform. In the colonies, the cost of equipping oneself was much less. A colonial militiaman wore his regular clothes and carried only a light musket, a tomahawk, and a scalping knife. Every able-bodied man from 16 to 60 years was required to serve in the colonial militia, although many avoided doing so by hiring a substitute or paying a fine. In addition, certain occupations—such as those of judge, minister, schoolmaster, miller, and miner—were exempt from service. Blacks, of course, were not allowed to become militiamen, nor were indentured servants.

In general, though, such violent uprisings were more the exception than the rule as many slaves strove to create a culture of their own. As they had children, many worked to create a stable family structure to sustain themselves and their offspring. Through patience, determination, and resiliency, African Americans developed an autonomous cultural space for themselves in the New World.

Freedom. Two legal means to freedom lay open to blacks. One was purchase, and slave artisans in particular were able to arrange to earn enough money to buy their liberty. The other

legal means was emancipation by an owner. In some colonies, this carried a price for the owner, who was required to post bond to guarantee against a former slave becoming a public charge.

Freedom was not an unalloyed blessing, though. Freed blacks with a skill were usually better off than those who had to rely on menial labor for a livelihood. However, barrel makers in New York were not the only white artisans who resented black competition. Free blacks were segregated in churches and schools. In New England they were required to carry a pass at all times and to observe curfew laws, and citizenship rights did not accompany freedom. For example, free blacks could not vote. Whether they lived in the North or in the South, African Americans, even though free, were viewed with suspicion in a predominantly white society. A black person anywhere was open to questioning, and the burden of proof of freedom rested on him or her. Lack of proof could mean a return to slavery.

Benjamin Banneker, the son of a freed slave, was probably the best-known black person in early United States history. He was an astronomer, farmer, mathematician, and surveyor. He helped draw up the plan for Washington, D.C. Phillis Wheatley, who was brought to Boston on a slave ship when she was about age eight, became a poet. In "To the Right Honorable William, Earl of Dartmouth," she contrasted her status as a slave with the American Colonies' demands for independence.

George Washington and his 10,000 men spent the winter of 1777 and 1778 camped at Valley Forge, Penn. It was a time of scarce food and poor conditions. By spring, about 2,500 of the men had died. Today, the campsite is a national historic park, and reenactments of the famous events are sometimes performed there.

Designed by George Washington, the badge of merit was awarded to soldiers who showed unusual courage in the Revolutionary War. Today, the award is known as the Purple Heart.

CHAPTER 15: WAR AND INDEPENDENCE

Wars for empire reminded the colonists that they were part of a larger world. As subjects of the British Crown, most believed they belonged to a homeland across the sea and possessed a stake in its fortunes. Wars between England and France were the product of fierce competition for economic advantage. Their repercussions were felt in the American Colonies and known by names such as King William's War and the French and Indian War.

Polish patriot and
engineer Thaddeus
Kosciusko used his
expertise to help the
Continental Army
during the war.
Later, he returned to
Poland and tried
unsuccessfully to
prevent the partition
of his homeland.

Just before the French and Indian
War began, a group of immigrants—
whose descendants are known today
as Cajuns—arrived from Acadia, in
Canada. Acadia had been settled by
the French but was taken over by the
British in 1713. However, the French
settlers refused to swear allegiance to
the British Crown. They wanted to be
neutral in any future conflict between
England and France.

In 1755, however, the British government—distrustful of the Acadians—forced some 10,000 men,
women, and children from their
farms at bayonet point, herded them
aboard ship, and dumped them in
the English colonies. Since the men
were deported first, families were separated, and many never saw their
loved ones again. However, a large
number of Acadians who were put

The Marquis de Lafayette saw the Revolutionary War as a chance to win military glory against Great Britain for France. At first, he did not impress the Americans very much, but his bold actions soon won him the respect he deserved, although he was not yet 24 years old. In 1784, he revisited America and stayed with President Washington at Mount Vernon. In 1803, America awarded Lafayette a huge amount of land in Louisiana, and in 1824, the U.S. Congress gave him $200,000 and land in Florida in gratitude for his help during the Revolutionary War.

ashore in Maryland and Virginia succeeded in making their way to French Louisiana (which became part of the United States in 1803). Their Cajun descendants still live in southern Louisiana and still speak a French-Canadian dialect. American poet Henry Wadsworth Longfellow described the event in his famous narrative poem "Evangeline."

The French and Indian War, or the Seven Years' War as it was known in Europe, was global in its scope. Early on, the French beat the British troops everywhere. It was only after William Pitt once again became prime minister that the tide turned in Britain's favor. The war ended with British victory at Quebec and Montreal. The peace treaty, signed in 1763, granted Britain almost all of Canada and most of the land in the Mississippi Valley and the Great Lakes region that France formerly controlled. The British and their colonists were now part of the mightiest empire in the world, and colonial power was at its peak. However there were costs as well as benefits.

The American Revolution Begins. War broke out in April 1775 when colonial troops and British regulars exchanged fire at Lexington, Mass.

Congress appointed George Washington commander in chief of American forces, and several outstanding European military officers came to America to aid in the fight against Great Britain. Thaddeus Kosciusko arrived from Poland in 1776, and Congress made him a colonel of engineers. Kosciusko directed the erection of fortifications at Saratoga, N.Y., where the Americans won an important victory. He was also responsible for fortifications along the Hudson River. After the war, Congress promoted Kosciusko to brigadier general.

The Marquis de Lafayette, who attended a French military academy at age 16, left France in 1777 when he was only 20 to volunteer for army service in America. Congress appointed him a major general, and he became an aide to George Washington. Lafayette was wounded at the battle of Brandywine in Pennsylvania in 1777 and spent part of the bitter winter of 1777–1778 at Valley Forge. He led troops in the battles of Barren Hill and Monmouth, N.J., and in campaigns against the British in Rhode Island. Returning to France early in 1779, he helped persuade the French government to aid the Patriot cause by sending both troops and supplies to the Americans. Lafayette was also a leader at the battle of Yorktown, which ended the fighting in 1781.

Casimir Pulaski, a Polish nobleman, was made a brigadier general in the Continental Army and assigned as an aide to General Washington. Pulaski fought in the battle of Brandywine and later organized a cavalry outfit known as Pulaski's Legion. In 1779, he was wounded during the American siege of Savannah and died two days later.

Baron von Steuben, a native of the German state of Prussia who fought in the Seven Years' War, arrived in America in 1777. He was made a major general and a member of Washington's staff. The commander in chief placed von Steuben in charge of teaching American soldiers close-order drill, marching, and the use of muskets and bayonets.

Von Steuben spoke French and German, but not English. So at first he communicated with his American troops by dictating orders in French, which one of Washington's officers wrote out and then translated into English. By "reading" the written orders and listening as someone pronounced the sounds, von Steuben learned the English words he needed to give commands. His broken English and explosive, profane German amused Washington's soldiers, but it was von Steuben who turned a ragtag bunch of colonials into a well-disciplined army capable of standing up to the best British regulars.

Von Steuben commanded troops at the battles of Monmouth and Yorktown. After the war he remained in America, retiring from army life to live in New York State.

Patriots and Loyalists.

Although a majority of the colonists supported calls for changes in British rules and laws, as many as a third of the people opposed a complete break with Great Britain. The other two-thirds were split between those who supported the Patriot cause, and those who preferred to remain neutral. Adherence to Loyalist beliefs cut across ethnic, economic, class, occupational, friendship, neighborhood, and family lines, as well as across geographic boundaries.

Some Loyalists were prosperous merchants, others were large landowners or eminent clergymen. For example Thomas Hutchinson, a former governor of Massachusetts,

and Joseph Galloway, a wealthy Philadelphia lawyer, were Loyalists as were members of their families. Benjamin Franklin was a Patriot. However, his son William, a governor of New Jersey, remained loyal to the Crown. Loyalists, though, were found not only among prominent citizens but also among carpenters, shoemakers, small farmers, teachers, and shopkeepers.

From the Patriot point of view, Loyalist opposition to a break with Britain was at best misguided, at worst traitorous. The common Patriot view of Loyalists was clear: "a man whose head was in England, his body in America and whose neck ought to be stretched." In fact, some necks *were* stretched, and a number of Loyalists

Polish nobleman Casimir Pulaski, shown here as he was fatally wounded at Savannah, has been honored by an act of the U.S. Congress that named October 11 as Pulaski Day.

DEATH OF PULASKI AT SAVANNAH

When Baron von Steuben arrived in Valley Forge on Feb. 23, 1778, and saw the suffering men of the Continental Army, he said that no European army could have held together in such circumstances. He quickly set about teaching the men to fight with the bayonets on their muskets and to march in a way that meant that the whole army could move much faster from place to place. Within a month, General Washington wrote that the army's prospects were beginning to improve.

were tarred and feathered. This severe form of punishment involved pouring hot tar on the offender's skin and could cause death.

Loyalists sometimes actively worked against the Patriot cause by spying, rounding up cattle and horses and supplies for the British, and organizing guerrilla bands. James DeLancey for example, was the wealthiest man in colonial New York and was a major political leader there before the revolution. He formed a mounted guerrilla band to keep supply routes open to the British occupying New York. Patriots captured him in November 1777 but then released him. DeLancey thereupon resumed his Loyalist ways, gathering another mounted troop to steal livestock for the British. In addition, it has been estimated that some 50,000 Loyalists served in British armies, plus 9,000 in special colonial units.

All immigrant groups could count members on both sides of the Revolutionary War, as well as in the middle. The Scotch-Irish in Pennsylvania overwhelmingly supported the Patriot cause, though the British there were able to recruit a regiment known as Volunteers of Ireland. The Irish formed the Loyal Irish Volunteers in Boston, a city which the British held at the beginning of the war. In North Carolina, South Carolina, and Georgia, many Scotch-Irish were Loyalists who favored the British cause.

Germans in Pennsylvania supported the Patriot side. Germans in Georgia, on the other hand, favored the Loyalists in what was really a civil war on the frontier between colonists on the coast and those in the interior.

Mercenaries, or soldiers who serve in a foreign army for money, came from Germany, many recruited from the province of Hesse to fight as regulars for the British. Congress sought to woo the Hessian soldiers away from the British by offering them free land. Thousands of Hessians accepted the offer, and an estimated 5,000 stayed in America after the war.

There were Loyalists as well as Patriots among the French Huguenot immigrants and among the Jews. However, the vast majority of both groups sided against the British.

Many of those who remained neutral in the conflict were members of religious groups that opposed all war on moral grounds. Among these peace sects were the Quakers, the Mennonites, the Dunkers, and the Shakers. The Schwenkfelders—a Protestant group in Pennsylvania—had no objection to supporting the Patriots financially with their taxes, but they *did* object to military service. In 1777, they issued a statement declaring that "for conscience's sake it is impossible for us to take up arms and kill our fellowmen," and added that all Schwenkfelders would contribute to a common fund for paying whatever fines might be imposed on conscientious objectors.

African Americans and the War. Enslaved African Americans had no enthusiasm for the Patriot cause nor any devotion to the British. Many however, saw the war as an opportunity to improve their lot by fighting for one or the other of the sides. Records are too scanty to reveal, though, how many black enlistees were slaves and how many were free. Both George Washington and the Continental Congress remained deaf to the idea of recruiting blacks for quite a while. The need for troops finally overcame their reluctance, though South Carolina and Georgia remained opposed throughout the war. In all, about 5,000 African Americans served on the American side.

In the Continental Army, many blacks were placed in labor battalions. However, African Americans served as fighting soldiers in some militia groups and saw action at Monmouth, Yorktown, and other battles. A number of blacks became sailors on American privateers. The British employed African Americans mainly as carpenters, blacksmiths, guides, and unskilled laborers.

The African-American contribution to the cause of independence did not necessarily alter European colonists' belief that blacks were an inferior people. One Pennsylvania soldier of European ancestry said:

But even in this regiment there were a number of Ne-

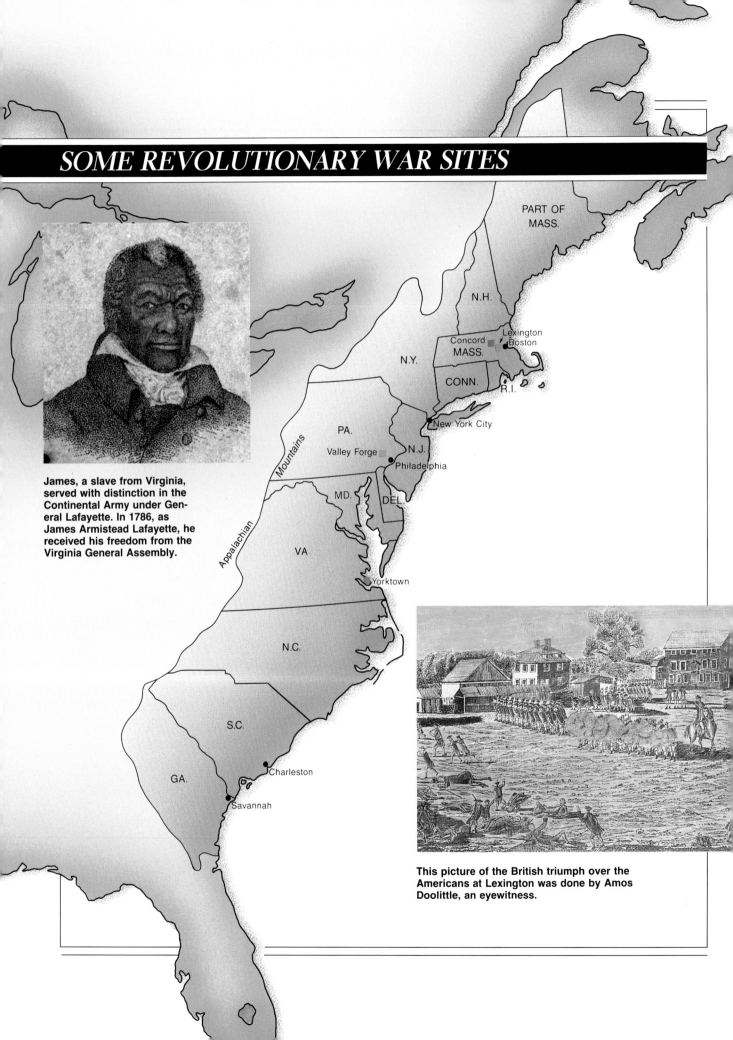

SOME REVOLUTIONARY WAR SITES

James, a slave from Virginia, served with distinction in the Continental Army under General Lafayette. In 1786, as James Armistead Lafayette, he received his freedom from the Virginia General Assembly.

PART OF MASS.

N.H.

N.Y.

Concord
MASS.
Lexington
Boston

CONN.

R.I.

New York City

PA.

Valley Forge

N.J.

Philadelphia

MD.

DEL.

VA.

Yorktown

N.C.

S.C.

Charleston

GA.

Savannah

Appalachian Mountains

This picture of the British triumph over the Americans at Lexington was done by Amos Doolittle, an eyewitness.

groes, which, to persons unaccustomed to such associations, had a disagreeable, degrading effect.

Exodus. During the war, state governments confiscated the Loyalists' property. Some 4,000 Loyalists filed claims for compensation with the British government, eventually receiving about a third of what they had asked for. During and after the war, emigration replaced immigration in America when as many as 100,000 Loyalists fled the country for

on the new nation after the war. When the British left Charleston, New York, and Savannah, several thousand African Americans sailed with them. The emigrant blacks found new homes in Canada and in the West Indies. In the West Indies, though, they were often sold again as slaves by the ships' captains.

"This is an American." The year before the peace treaty ending the Revolutionary War was signed, a French-born immigrant named Guillaume Jean de Crèvecoeur wrote *Let-*

During and after the war, emigration replaced immigration in America when as many as 100,000 Loyalists fled the country . . . .

Canada, the Bahamas, other British territories, and England itself.

Leaving home was not easy. Thomas Hutchinson, one of those who chose exile, probably spoke for many when he wrote:

My thoughts day and night are upon New England. . . . I had rather die in a little country farm house in N. England than in the best Nobleman's seat in Old England.

About the same time, a colonist from Rhode Island probably also expressed the thoughts of many when he wrote from Nova Scotia:

A whole Continent ruined. . . . I could freely give up my Life, and Ten Thousand more if I possessed them, could I restore dear Rhode Island to its former happy, happy Situation.

Several thousand blacks, many of them slaves, also turned their backs

ters from an American Farmer, a book in which he asked: "What then is the American, this new man?" He answered his own question this way:

Americans are the western pilgrims, who are carrying along with them that great mass of arts, sciences, vigour, and industry which began long since in the east; they will finish the great circle. . . . The American is a new man, who acts upon new principles . . . From involuntary idleness, servile dependence, penury, [poverty], and useless labour, he has passed to toils of a very different nature, rewarded by ample subsistence.—This is an American.

Women, Indians, and blacks did not fall within Crèvecoeur's definition of an American. For these groups, full citizenship was a long way off.

The earliest history of Canada was much like that of the United States. The first immigrants came across the Bering Strait into the new land at least 20,000 years ago.

rival of France for land in America. The conflict finally ended in the 1760's with a British victory. Great Britain then ruled over the relatively small but fiercely proud group of French-Catholic

Loyalists from the American colonies migrated to Canada. The increased number of British Loyalists soon led to both cultural and political friction with Canada's French-speaking population.

Constitutional Act of 1791, which split Quebec into two colonies. The area along the lower St. Lawrence River became known as Lower Canada and was inhabited mostly by the French-speaking population. The area near the Great Lakes and the upper

CANADA: A DIFFERENT STORY

Early Years.
About A.D. 1000, Eric the Red and some other Viking explorers landed on the coast of North America. The remains of a Viking settlement can still be seen today near what is now St. Lunaire, Newfoundland. One of the next Europeans, Italian navigator John Cabot, arrived in 1497. French fur traders and fishers followed in the 1500's. Then in 1608, Samuel de Champlain of France founded one of the first European settlements—Quebec—on the St. Lawrence River. This became the nucleus of the colony of New France.

Life in the 1600's and 1700's.
In the 1600's, England became a great

settlers who valued their heritage and were determined to preserve it.

To calm French-Canadian fears, the British Parliament passed the Quebec Act in 1774. This law recognized French civil and religious rights and preserved the land ownership system the French had developed in Canada.

During the American Revolution, many Canadians remained loyal to Britain, and after the war, some 40,000

The new arrivals demanded the kind of self-government they had known before. Britain responded with the

Shown in this painting is African American clergyman and teacher Josiah Henson, who fled from America to Canada in 1830. Henson was the basis for one of the characters in *Uncle Tom's Cabin*.

In 1790, British officer Thomas Davies painted this view of a Canadian farm and its surroundings. Davies called the work *View of the Bridge on Rivière La Puce*.

Russian immigrant Casimir Gzowski, shown here with his family, played key roles in the construction of Canada's railway system and the International Bridge between Fort Erie, Ont., and Buffalo, N.Y.

St. Lawrence became known as Upper Canada and was inhabited mainly by English-speaking people.

Life in the 1800's. During the War of 1812, Canadian militias joined British regulars to repel an American invasion, and this boosted feelings of patriotism and loyalty in Canada. After the war, however, the French-Canadian apprehension grew as immigrants from England, Ireland, and Scotland swelled the English-speaking population.

The anxiety of French Canadians increased further as the British settlers gained control of both Upper Canada and Lower Canada. These anxieties, as well as dissatisfaction with the colonial governments in general, led to rebellions in both Upper and Lower Canada in 1837 and 1838. The uprisings were easily put down, but they demonstrated to the British that important changes were needed. In 1840, Upper Canada and Lower Canada were combined into the Province of Canada. However, many of the long-standing problems remained.

Finally in 1867, the British Parliament passed the British North America Act, which established the Dominion of Canada. The four initial provinces—New Brunswick, Nova Scotia, Ontario, and Quebec—each received some rights of self-government. Great Britain kept control of foreign affairs, and the British monarch remained the head of state.

Westward expansion led to serious problems in the Canadian Northwest. By 1869, the 12,000 European settlers in the area had arranged their landholdings according to the old French plan of strips reaching back from the riverfronts. When newly chosen British officials decided to rearrange things, the settlers rose up in revolt. This Red

In 1854, Timothy Eaton emigrated from Ireland to Canada. He later founded what became Canada's largest privately owned department store.

Born in Illinois, Sir William Van Horne became general manager of the Canadian Pacific Railroad in 1882 and used his skills to push completion of the main line. The main line completion helped immigrants, such as these camped along the railroad line, prosper in Alberta and Saskatchewan.

During World War II, Canada detained its citizens of Japanese descent in camps in Greenwood, B.C., shown above, and in six other locations.

River Rebellion of 1869 was led by Louis Riel. Most of the rebels, including Riel, were *métis*—persons of mixed European and Indian ancestry. At first, the government agreed to many of the rebel demands. Then Riel pushed too hard. The uprising eventually failed, and Riel was hanged in 1885. Many of the rebels left their Red River Valley homes in the newly created Province of Manitoba and moved farther west-ward into what later became the Province of Saskatchewan.

Life after 1900. In World War II, Canadians of Japanese ancestry suffered much the same racist treatment as their fellow Japanese in the United States. In Canada—as in the United States—people of Japanese descent were forced into internment

The huge nation of Canada is the world's second largest in land area.

- Dawson
YUKON TERRITORY
★ Whitehorse
NORTHWEST TERRITORIES
★ Yellowknife
NUNAVUT
★ Iqaluit
NEWFOUNDLAND AND LABRADOR
BRITISH COLUMBIA
Churchill •
• Gander
St. John's
ALBERTA
Edmonton ★
MANITOBA
QUEBEC
PRINCE EDWARD ISLAND
Victoria ★ • Vancouver
SASKATCHEWAN
Saskatoon •
Fredericton ★
★ Charlottetown
NOVA SCOTIA
• Calgary
★ Regina
ONTARIO
Quebec ★
★ Halifax
★ Winnipeg
Thunder Bay •
NEW BRUNSWICK
Montreal •
Ottawa ★
Toronto ★
London • • Hamilton
Windsor

camps despite no evidence of misdeeds.

After World War II, Canada accepted many European war refugees. Somewhat later, it accepted several thousand refugees from Southeast Asia.

Issues relating to the treatment of French Canadians continue to be a source of anxiety and unrest. In the 1960's, a Quebec separatist movement began. However, in 1980, about 60 per cent of Quebec voters refused to endorse separatism.

In 1980, the Canadian government changed the national anthem from "God Save the Queen" to "O Canada." Then in 1982, Canada revised its constitution, and the Quebec problem arose again. Quebec refused to accept the new constitution, saying it did not give enough protection to and recognition of French-Canadian culture of the nation.

In 1987, a constitutional amendment—the Meech Lake Accord—was proposed, granting special rights to Quebec, including recognition of it as a "distinct society" within Canada. However, the amendment did not pass.

Critics protested that the proposed amendment gave Quebec's provincial government too much power. They also pointed out that the agreement made provisions for the French-Canadian minority but not for any other minority within the country.

After the failure of the accord, many Quebecers began to demand independence from the rest of Canada. In October 1995, Quebec voters narrowly defeated a referendum that would have granted independence for Quebec, and the province remained part of Canada. In late 1995, Parliament passed a resolution recognizing Quebec's unique language, culture, and civil law.

Today, Canada's population is more than 31 million. About a third of the people have some English ancestry, and about a fourth have some French ancestry. Other large groups include German, Scottish, and Irish immigrants and their descendants. In addition, many Asian immigrants live in Ontario and in western Canada. The first settlers—the Eskimos and the Indians—make up only about 2 per cent of Canada's population now.

In the 1930's, Jewish scientist Gerhard Herzberg emigrated from Europe to Canada to escape the persecution of Jews that Hitler was waging there. In 1971, Herzberg won the Nobel Prize for his work in molecular spectroscopy, becoming Canada's third Nobel laureate.

Today, some of Canada's Inuit continue to make decorated clothing and other artistic items using the methods and designs of their ancestors.

As in America, many of Canada's immigrants have become leading citizens. Armenian immigrant Yousuf Karsh is known worldwide for his portraits of famous people such as Winston Churchill. Dancer Celia Franca emigrated from England and founded the National Ballet of Canada.

ACKNOWLEDGMENTS

All World Book maps were created especially for this volume by John M. Isard and Roberta Polfus.

COVER: © Corbis/Bettmann
1 © Susan Middleton, California Academy of Sciences; Granger Collection
4 © Owen Franken, Stock, Boston
6 W. Perry Conway, Tom Stack & Assoc.
8 Tom Bean, DRK: Claude Steelman, Tom Stack & Assoc.; Harold E. Wilson, Earth Scenes
9 Tom and Pat Leeson, DRK
10 Brian Milne, Animals Animals; Johnny Johnson, DRK
12 Michael Fogden, Oxford Scientific Films from Earth Scenes
13 Gerald A. Corsi, Tom Stack & Assoc.; SuperStock
14 Steven Fuller, Earth Scenes
15 Tom Bean, DRK
16 Tom Algire, Tom Stack & Assoc.
17 Wayne Lynch, DRK
18 M. Timothy O'Keefe, Tom Stack & Assoc.; Byron Augustin, Tom Stack & Assoc.
19 Mike Andrews, Animals Animals
20 Jerry Jacka; Denver Art Museum; Jill and Peter Furst
21 Museum of the American Indian
23 American Museum of Natural History (Lee Boltin); Jill and Peter Furst
24 Denver Museum of Natural History; Museum of New Mexico
25 Warren Morgan; University Museum, Philadelphia (World Book photo by Robert Crandall)
26 John W. Warden
27 Chuck Place
28 David Muench
28 Pansy Stockton Collection (Laura Gilpin)
30–31 National Museum of American Art (Art Resource)
32 Tony Linck
33 Stock Montage
34 Cahokia Mounds State Historic Site
35 Cahokia Mounds State Historic Site; Jill and Peter Furst
36 Loren McIntyre; Lee Boltin
37 Jill and Peter Furst
39 Dale E. Boyer, Photo Researchers
40 Jill and Peter Furst, Ulrike Welsch, Photo Researchers
41 © Nefsky (Art Resource); Lee Boltin; Firenze Museo di Anthropologia (Art Resource)
42 Jill and Peter Furst
43 Hamilton Wright, Photo Researchers; Lee Boltin
44 Lee Boltin
46 National Maritime Museum
48 Museo Naval; Susan Middleton, California Academy of Sciences; Bettmann
49 © Aldus Books (John Webb); Granger Collection
50 Mitte Foto A/S
51 Granger Collection
52 Mansell Collection
53 Smithsonian Institution
54 Granger Collection
56 Metropolitan Museum of Art, Gift of J. Pierpont Morgan, 1900
58 Jerry Howard, Stock, Boston; Culver; Granger Collection
59 Culver
60 Biblioteca Nacional, Madrid (MAS)
61 Library of Congress
63 Royal Ontario Museum, Toronto (World Book

photo); Stock Montage
64 Huntington Library, San Marino, California
65 Culver; New York City Art Commission
66–67 Granger Collection
68 Tony Pacheco; Lee Foster, Bruce Coleman Inc.
69 Field Museum of Natural History, Chicago (World Book photo); James Cowlin
70 Nuestra Senora de Copacabana, Lima, Peru (Jose Casals)
71 The Hispanic Society of America, New York
72 © The Pierpont Morgan Library 1991, #MA3900 f.103
73 © The Pierpont Morgan Library 1991, #MA3900 f.97
74 Lee Boltin; The Hispanic Society of America, New York; The Hispanic Society of America, New York
76 Granger Collection
77 Elliot Erwitt, Magnum
78 MAS
79 V. C. Lefteroff, Superstock
82 National Archives of Canada, #C-11743
83 National Archives of Canada, #C-15791; Thomas Gilcrease Institute of American History and Art
84 Library of Congress
85 New York Public Library
86 Hudson's Bay Company; National Gallery of Canada
87 National Archives of Canada, #C-7300
88 Library of Congress
90 Granger Collection
91 National Archives of Canada, #C-788
92 © Corbis/Bettmann; Museum of the City of New York; Cats Wercken, 1658
93 Culver
95 Library of Congress
96 American Swedish Historical Museum
97 Metropolitan Museum of Art
98 Metropolitan Museum of Art, Robert Lehman Collection, 1975
99 Granger Collection; National Gallery, London
100 © Farrell Grehan
102 © Farrell Grehan, Photo Researchers; © Corbis/Bettmann; Granger Collection
103 Granger Collection
105 Generall Historie of Virginia, 1624
106 Andrew W. Mellon Collection, National Portrait Gallery
107–108 © Corbis/Bettmann
109 AP/Wide World; The Pilgrim Society
110 Granger Collection
111 The Pilgrim Society
112–113 Plimoth Plantation Inc., Plymouth, Massachusetts
114 Maryland Historical Society; Bettmann; Essex Institute, Salem, Massachusetts, #16,009
115 Granger Collection
116 M. and M. Karolik Collection of American Paintings, Museum of Fine Arts, Boston; Granger Collection
117 © Free Chin
118–119 Granger Collection
121 Thomas Gilcrease Institute of American History and Art; Historical Society of Pennsylvania

122 Museum of Fine Arts, Boston
123 New York Public Library; Maryland Historical Society
124 New York Public Library
125 Colonial Williamsburg; Culver
126 British Museum
128 Salem History Society
129 Sutro Library
130 © Free Chin; Dorset Natural History and Archaeological Society, Dorset County Museum, Dorchester, Dorset
132 Massachusetts Historical Society
134 Museum of American Folk Art; © Free Chin; Old Salem, Inc.
135 Historical Society of York County
137 Colonial Williamsburg Foundation
138 Titus C. Geesey Collection, Philadelphia Museum of Art; Historical Society of York County
139 State Museum of Pennsylvania/Pennsylvania Historical and Museum Commission
140 American Jewish Historical Society; The Society of Friends Touro Synagogue, Newport, R.I.
142 World Book file
143 Worcester College, Oxford University
144 Charleston Museum, Charleston, South Carolina; Connecticut Historical Society; © Corbis/Bettmann
145 Library Company of Philadelphia
147 Marblehead Historical Society; Library of Congress
148 Sea Captains Carousing in Surinam, an oil painting on bed ticking by John Greenwood, Museum Purchase, Saint Louis Art Museum
150 Metropolitan Museum of Art, Gift of Edgar William and Bernice Chrysler Garbisch, 1963
151 South Caroliniana Library
152 National Maritime Museum
153 © Corbis/Bettmann; American Antiquarian Society
155 Newberry Library
156 Charleston Museum, Charleston, South Carolina
157 Huntington Library, San Marino, California
158 Maryland Historical Society
159 Maryland Historical Society; © Corbis/Bettmann
160 National Park Service; © Ted Spiegel, Black Star; Valley Forge Historical Society
161 © Corbis/Bettmann
162 Washington, Curtis, Lee Collection, Washington and Lee University
163 FDR Library
164 Pennsylvania Capitol Preservation Committee; Titus C. Geesey Collection, Philadelphia Museum of Art
166 Virginia Historical Society; Connecticut Historical Society
168 Upper Canada Village, St. Lawrence Parks Commission; National Gallery of Canada, Ottawa
169 Archives of Ontario, #S.4308; National Archives of Canada, #PA-038667; National Archives of Canada, #C-8549; Eaton's of Canada
170 National Archives of Canada, #C24452; J. Feeney, NFB Collection, Canadian Museum of Contemporary Photography
171 National Research Council, Canada; Duncan Cameron, National Archives of Canada, #PA-123846; National Ballet of Canada Archive

INDEX

Note: Page numbers in **bold face** are references to illustrations.